MOCKTAILS MADE EASY:
HOW TO CRAFT HEALTHY & DELICIOUS NON-ALCOHOLIC DRINKS FOR EVERY OCCASION

108+ SIMPLE RECIPES USING EVERYDAY INGREDIENTS

ERIC SANTAGADA

© Copyright Eric Santagada 2024 - All rights reserved.

The content within this book may not be reproduced, duplicated, or transmitted without direct written permission from the author or the publisher.

Under no circumstances will any blame or legal responsibility be held against the publisher or author for any damages, reparation, or monetary loss due to the information contained within this book. Either directly or indirectly. You are responsible for your own choices, actions, and results.

Legal Notice:

This book is copyright-protected. This book is only for personal use. You cannot amend, distribute, sell, use, quote, or paraphrase any part of this book's content without the author's or publisher's consent.

Disclaimer Notice:

Please note the information contained within this document is for educational and entertainment purposes only. All effort has been expended to present accurate, up-to-date, and reliable, complete information. No warranties of any kind are declared or implied. Readers acknowledge that the author is not engaging in the rendering of legal, financial, medical or professional advice. The content within this book has been derived from various sources. Please consult a licensed professional before attempting any techniques outlined in this book.

By reading this document, the reader agrees that under no circumstances is the author responsible for any losses, direct or indirect, which are incurred as a result of the use of the information contained within this document, including, but not limited to, — errors, omissions, or inaccuracies.

CONTENTS

Introduction — 5

1. GETTING STARTED WITH MOCKTAILS — 9
   1.1 The Art of Mocktails: An Overview — 9
   1.2 Common Ingredients: What You Need in Your Pantry — 11
   1.3 Understanding Flavor Profiles and Combinations — 13
   1.4 Essential Tools & Techniques — 15
   1.5 Sweeteners: Simple Syrup, Honey, Agave, and More — 19
   1.6 Encouraging a Sober Lifestyle through Mocktails — 21

2. SEASONAL MOCKTAILS — 25
   2.1 Springtime Fresh: Floral and Herbal Mocktails — 25
   2.2 Summer Harvest: Fruit-Forward Mocktails — 30
   2.3 Autumn Flavors: Spiced and Cozy Mocktails — 35
   2.4 Winter Warmers: Comforting Mocktail Recipes — 39
   2.5 Farm-to-Glass: Sourcing Seasonal & Local Ingredients — 42
   2.6 Zero-Waste & Eco-Friendly Practices in Mixology — 44

3. MOCKTAILS FOR SOCIAL GATHERINGS — 49
   3.1 Sophisticated Sippers — 49
   3.2 Large Batch Mocktails for Parties — 53
   3.3 Elegant Brunch Mocktails — 56
   3.4 Mocktails for Dinner Parties — 60
   3.5 Quick and Easy Mocktails for Last-Minute Guests — 63

4. MOCKTAILS FOR SPECIAL OCCASIONS — 69
   4.1 Holiday-Themed Mocktails — 69
   4.2 Birthday Bash Mocktails — 73

4.3 Wedding and Baby Shower Mocktails 76
4.4 Festive Mocktails for New Year's Eve 80

5. FAMILY-FRIENDLY MOCKTAILS 85
5.1 Fizzy Fruit Punches 85
5.2 Creative Lemonades and Limeades 88
5.3 Kid-Friendly Smoothies and Shakes 92
5.4 Popsicles: Refreshing Treats 95

6. HEALTH-CONSCIOUS MOCKTAILS 99
6.1 Fruit Infusions 99
6.2 Herbal and Botanical Blends 101
6.3 Superfood Smoothies: Nutrient-Rich Options 104
6.4 Detoxifying Mocktails 106
6.5 Immune-Boosting Mocktails 108
6.6 Digestive Health: Mocktails for Gut Wellness 110
6.7 Energy-Boosting Mocktails 112

7. PREGNANCY-SAFE MOCKTAILS 115
7.1 Nourishing Smoothies for Moms-to-Be 115
7.2 Herbal Teas and Infusions for Pregnancy 118
7.3 Mocktails Rich in Vitamins and Minerals 121

8. ADVANCED MIXOLOGY TECHNIQUES 125
8.1 Crafting Infusions and Syrups 125
8.2 Advanced Garnishing Techniques 128
8.3 Layering and Presentation Mastery 130
8.4 Fermented and Probiotic Mocktails 132
8.6 The Role of Texture in Mocktails 135
8.7 Understanding Acidity and Balance in Drinks 137

Conclusion 139
References 145

INTRODUCTION

A few years ago, on a warm summer evening, I attended a garden party hosted by a friend. The scene was idyllic, with twinkling lights between the trees and laughter filling the air. Navigating the social maze, I felt a pang of discomfort. I had recently gone sober, and the sight of clinking glasses brimming with wine and cocktails reminded me of past challenges. Just then, a server approached with a tray of non-alcoholic drinks, and I chose a vibrant, refreshing mocktail.

With my first sip, everything changed. The drink was a delightful mix of tangy lime, fresh mint, and sweet agave syrup—crisp, clean, and invigorating. I felt a sense of belonging, contentment, and tranquility as I enjoyed the beverage. That moment ignited a passion for creating mocktails that aren't merely alternatives to alcohol but celebrations in their own right.

This book is the result of that inspiration. It serves as your guide to crafting healthy and delicious mocktails for any occasion. Whether you're hosting a dinner party, celebrating holidays with loved ones, or enjoying a quiet night at home, this book will provide the mixology skills to create stunning, satisfying drinks with whatever ingredients you have.

Let's take a quick dive into the book's layout. The chapters are grouped by theme, offering everything from easy to complex recipes. You'll discover personal stories, helpful tips, and plenty of illustrations along the way. Each chapter blends hands-on guidance with inspiring narratives to create a truly engaging experience.

For example, Chapter Two, "Seasonal Mocktails," highlights the unique flavors of each season, from refreshing summer coolers to warming winter brews. Chapter Three, "Mocktails for Social Hosts," delves into drink ideas perfect for celebrations, complete with tips on presentation and pairing with food. Chapter Six focuses on "Health-Conscious Mocktails," offering a range of functional recipes you can make with ingredients you likely already have at home.

Let me tell you a little about my journey. In my 20s, I was a professional musician who struggled with substance abuse. At the time, I knew I needed a profound shift to break free from my downward spiral. My life took a drastic change when I decided to go sober and immersed myself in personal development books, yoga, meditation, and prayer. Eventually, I moved into an ashram and embraced the life of a monk, where cooking with love and devotion became part of my spiritual practice. As an author and speaker, I am passionate about inspiring others on their path to health, happiness, and selfless service.

These experiences have profoundly influenced my approach to mixing non-alcoholic drinks. Every mocktail is crafted with intention and offered with love, aiming to bring joy and wellness to those who partake. The recipes in this book are straightforward, with detailed instructions that anyone can understand and replicate.

Instead of full-page recipes and glitzy photos, we packed as much content as possible into this book, opting for black-and-white printing and simple illustrations to keep costs low and pass the savings on to you.

I invite you to experiment with each recipe, embrace your creativity, and enjoy the process of making and sharing mocktails. This book is here to guide you, but it's your personal touch that will make each drink truly special. Cheers to new beginnings and the endless possibilities they bring!

GETTING STARTED WITH MOCKTAILS

1.1 THE ART OF MOCKTAILS: AN OVERVIEW

Mocktails, or non-alcoholic cocktails, have been gaining significant traction as more people embrace a healthier, sober lifestyle. These drinks mimic the complexity and elegance of traditional cocktails, minus the alcohol. The history of mocktails dates back to the Prohibition era of the 1920s when  bartenders got creative with non-alcoholic ingredients. Over time, they evolved from simple juice blends to sophisticated beverages that can stand alone at any social event or restaurant. Today, the rise of the sober-curious movement has further fueled the popularity of mocktails. More people are seeking ways to enjoy social gatherings without the adverse effects of alcohol.

Mocktails come in various forms, each offering a unique drinking experience. Refreshing coolers featuring cucumber, mint, and citrus ingredients are perfect for hot summer days. These drinks are light, hydrating, and incredibly refreshing. Creamy shakes take a different approach, often incorporating ingredients like coconut milk, yogurt, and fruit to create rich, indulgent beverages that can double as a dessert. Herbal infusions bring nature's complexity to your glass, using herbs like basil, rosemary, and lavender to add aromatic depth. Sparkling blends combine fruit juices, syrups, and carbonated water to create effervescent drinks that are both festive and satisfying.

A mocktail's visual appearance can significantly enhance the drinking experience. Colorful ingredients like fresh fruits, herbs, and edible flowers can make your mocktails visually stunning. Elegant glassware can transform a simple drink into a sophisticated pleasure. Consider using highball glasses for tall drinks, martini glasses for more refined beverages, or even mason jars for a rustic touch. Creative garnishes, such as citrus twists, herb sprigs, or even a rim of flavored salt or sugar, can elevate the presentation and make your mocktails look as good as they taste.

As you navigate this book, you'll find our approach to making mocktails lighthearted, spontaneous, and fun. The recipes are simple and effective, using common ingredients you can find easily at your local grocery store. We encourage you to experiment and be creative. Whether you're a novice or an experienced mixologist, this book offers something for everyone, from the basics to more advanced techniques.

Mocktails are more than just drinks; they are a statement. They represent a choice to live a healthy life, to celebrate without relying on alcohol, and to enjoy the finer things more consciously. This book is your guide to crafting these delightful beverages, and

I hope it inspires you to explore the endless possibilities of mocktail making.

1.2 COMMON INGREDIENTS: WHAT YOU NEED IN YOUR PANTRY

Crafting delicious and healthy mocktails starts with gathering the right ingredients. To ensure you're well-prepared, begin by stocking your pantry with fresh fruits, vegetables, herbs, spices, and natural sweeteners. Many mocktail recipes rely heavily on fresh produce as their foundation. Citrus fruits—such as lemons, limes, and oranges—deliver a bright, acidic punch, while berries, melons, and tropical fruits like pineapple and mango introduce sweetness and layers of flavor. For a refreshing twist, vegetables like cucumber and celery add a delightful crunch. Aromatic herbs, including mint, basil, and rosemary, contribute complexity, while spices like ginger and cinnamon infuse warmth and depth.

Natural sweeteners are crucial to balance the flavors in your mocktails. Honey and agave syrup are fantastic options, as they provide just the right amount of sweetness without the overwhelming taste of refined sugar. For an extra dimension, consider using maple syrup or simple syrups infused with herbs or spices, adding delightful flavor layers. When it comes to fizz, sparkling water and sodas are must-haves. They elevate a basic fruit juice into a refreshing, bubbly treat, making your drinks perfect for any celebration.

Every ingredient contributes significantly to the overall profile of a mocktail. Citrus fruits, for example, brighten recipes with their tangy flavors, delivering the acidity needed to balance out sweetness while adding a refreshing zest. Meanwhile, herbs bring aromatic intensity and richness—mint offers a cooling sensation, basil introduces a hint of pepper, and rosemary delivers a piney, earthy fragrance. Sweeteners serve a balancing role as well. Honey imparts a subtle floral essence, while agave syrup provides a gentler touch. Finally, bitters can round out a drink by adding depth and complexity.

Certain ingredients are exceptionally versatile. Lemons and limes are handy in everything from simple lemonades to complex herbal infusions. Mint and basil can be muddled into drinks or used as garnishes. If you're looking for warmth and spice, ginger and cinnamon are ideal choices. These ingredients can be mixed and matched in countless ways to create various flavors and experiences.

Proper storage of ingredients is critical to maintaining their freshness and quality. You should store fresh fruits and vegetables in the refrigerator to extend their shelf life. I prefer to keep herbs fresh by placing them in a glass of water in the fridge and covering them loosely with a plastic bag. Airtight containers are essential for storing natural sweeteners and spices, preventing them from absorbing moisture and losing their potency. Knowing the shelf-life of different ingredients can also help you plan your shopping and storage. For example, citrus fruits can last up to two weeks in the fridge, while herbs keep for about a week. Sweeteners like honey and agave syrup have a longer shelf life but should be kept in a cool, dark place to maintain quality.

Imagine hosting a summer barbecue with a refreshing cucumber mint cooler as the star of the show. The crispness of cucumber, the cooling effect of mint, and the brightness of lime come together to create a hydrating and delicious drink. Or picture a cozy winter

 evening with a spiced apple cider, where warm cinnamon and sweet honey make each sip a comforting delight. These experiences are made possible by having a well-stocked pantry with fresh, versatile ingredients.

1.3 UNDERSTANDING FLAVOR PROFILES AND COMBINATIONS

Creating a well-balanced mocktail starts with understanding flavor profiles. These profiles are the different tastes that make up our sensory experiences: sweet, sour, bitter, salty, astringent, and umami. Each profile plays a unique role in building a drink that is not only complex but also harmonious.

Sweetness can come from fruits, honey, or syrups and balances the tartness in a drink. Sour elements, often derived from citrus fruits like lemon and lime, provide a refreshing zing. Bitterness adds depth and sophistication through ingredients like tonic water, bitters, or certain herbs. Salt, though not always obvious, can enhance other flavors and create a more rounded profile. Astringent ingredients, such as leafy greens and some teas, cause a dry, puckering sensation in the mouth. Finally, umami, a savory taste that adds body to a drink, can be achieved through ingredients like tomatoes or fermented sauces. The key to a balanced mocktail is harmonizing these diverse flavors to create an intriguing and satisfying beverage.

Some flavor combinations have stood the test of time, offering a reliable foundation for any mocktail enthusiast. Citrus and mint are a classic pairing that combines the bright acidity of citrus fruits with the refreshing coolness of mint. Another famous duo is berries and basil. The sweetness and slight tartness of berries are complemented by the herbaceous notes of basil, creating a refreshing and complex drink. Ginger and lime is another dynamic pairing, offering a mix of spice and zest. In this combination, ginger's warmth brightens up lime's tartness. Lastly, cucumber and melon provide a mild, refreshing profile perfect for hot summer days.

By experimenting with these and other flavors, you can find delightful discoveries of your own. Start by keeping a flavor journal to note down successful combinations and any tweaks you make to a recipe. Taking notes helps in understanding what works and why. Small batch testing is another effective method. By creating smaller quantities, you can experiment freely without fearing waste. This approach allows you to balance bold and subtle flavors, giving you the freedom to explore different ingredients and techniques. For instance, you might find that adding a pinch of salt to a citrus-based drink enhances its brightness, or that a touch of honey can soften the bitterness of certain herbs. Experimentation broadens your skills and makes creating mocktails more enjoyable and personalized.

Balance is crucial in any mocktail. Adjusting sweetness and acidity can significantly change the final taste. If a drink is too sour, some sweetener can mellow it out. Conversely, if it's too sweet, a splash of citrus can add the necessary tartness. Using a pinch of salt can also enhance flavors, making them more pronounced and well-rounded. It's about finding the proper equilibrium between strong and mild ingredients to create a complex and satisfying drink.

Understanding and mastering flavor profiles and combinations will expand the possibilities of mocktail making. Whether you're hosting a party, enjoying an evening with your kids, or exploring new ways to stay healthy, these principles will guide you in creating delicious and balanced drinks. The joy of mocktail making lies in the endless opportunities for creativity and experimentation, allowing you to craft beverages that are uniquely yours.

1.4 ESSENTIAL TOOLS & TECHNIQUES

Creating great mocktails isn't just about the ingredients you use. Having the right tools and knowing how to use them is also essential. Proper equipment makes the preparation process smoother, more efficient, and ultimately more enjoyable. If you don't already own some of these, you can find them at a kitchen store or online retailer.

Let's start with the basics. A cocktail shaker is indispensable for blending ingredients seamlessly. Whether a Boston shaker or a cobbler shaker, this tool helps mix your mocktail ingredients, ensuring a uniform taste in every sip. When it's time to combine citrus juices, herbal syrups, and sparkling water, a quick, vigorous shake transforms these components into a harmonious blend, ready to be poured over ice.

Shaking brings a dynamic aspect to your mocktail-making. This method is perfect for drinks that require thorough mixing or need to be chilled quickly. To shake a mocktail, start by filling your cocktail shaker halfway with ice. Add ingredients, secure the lid, and shake vigorously for 15-20 seconds. The shaking action chills the drink rapidly and helps to incorporate air, giving it a frothy texture. Beverages that benefit from shaking include those with fruit juices, dairy, or syrups, such as a citrus cooler or a creamy piña colada mocktail. The benefits of shaking extend beyond mere mixing; it also alters the texture and mouthfeel of the drink, making it more refreshing and lively. Tightly seal the shaker to avoid spills, and use fresh ice for the best results.

Next on the list is the muddler. This simple tool is essential for crushing fruits, herbs, and spices to release their flavors. Imagine a summer evening when you're preparing a strawberry basil mocktail. By muddling strawberries and basil leaves at the bottom of your glass, you infuse your drink with fresh, aromatic flavor. The result is a mocktail that's not only delicious but also rich in texture and complexity.

Muddling is one of the foundational techniques in making mocktails. This process involves gently pressing and twisting ingredients at the bottom of a glass to release their essential oils and juices. Place your ingredients—fresh herbs, citrus slices, or berries—into the glass. Using a muddler, press down gently and give a slight twist. The goal is to bruise the ingredients, not pulverize them, which releases their flavors without creating an overly mushy texture. Herbs like mint and basil, citrus fruits like lemons and limes, and berries like strawberries and blueberries are ideal for muddling. One common mistake is applying too much pressure, which can result in a bitter taste, especially with herbs.

Another is muddling too long, which can break down the ingredients too much. By mastering the right amount of pressure and time, you can extract the maximum flavor without compromising the quality of your drink.

A jigger is another vital tool for any mocktail enthusiast. This small, dual-sided measuring device ensures you get the correct proportions of each ingredient, maintaining consistency in taste. Whether you're crafting a mocktail for yourself or a dozen guests, the jigger helps you measure everything from lime juice to agave syrup precisely. This precision guarantees that every drink you make is balanced, neither too sweet nor too tart.

Strainers are equally important, especially when you want a smooth, refined mocktail. After shaking or muddling, you must often separate the liquid from solid ingredients like fruit pulp or herb leaves. A fine-mesh or Hawthorne strainer does the job perfectly, allowing only the liquid to pass through while keeping the solids out. This step is crucial for creating clean, visually appealing mocktails that are a joy to drink.

In addition to these essentials, there are optional tools that can elevate your mocktail-making experience. A bar spoon, for instance, is perfect for gently stirring drinks without diluting or aerating them too much. This method is ideal for drinks that require a smooth, balanced texture, such as a herbal infusion or a sparkling blend. The goal is to mix the ingredients thoroughly while keeping the drink clear and free from air bubbles. Stirring blends the flavors and maintains the drink's clarity and consistency, making it visually appealing.

A citrus juicer is another handy tool that quickly extracts juice from lemons, limes, and oranges. It ensures the maximum amount of juice with minimal effort and saves time when making multiple drinks.

Blenders can also be helpful, especially for creamy shakes and smoothies. They help you achieve a smooth, frothy texture by blending ingredients thoroughly. Picture making a tropical mango coconut smoothie. A blender ensures the mango, coconut milk, and ice blend into a silky, luscious drink.

Ice molds can add a touch of elegance to your mocktails. Large, slow-melting ice cubes or decorative ice shapes keep your drink cold and enhance its visual appeal.

Investing in quality tools can make a significant difference in preparing and presenting your mocktails. High-quality tools are durable, often lasting for years, and perform better than their cheaper counterparts, making your job easier. For example, a well-made cocktail shaker will seal tightly, preventing leaks while you shake. A sturdy muddler will withstand the pressure needed to crush ingredients effectively. Good-quality tools are also more comfortable, reducing strain and making the experience more enjoyable. When your tools work well, you can focus on creativity and experimentation, knowing that the technical aspects are covered. High-quality tools contribute to the overall experience, making your creation process a fun time to share with family and friends.

Combining these tools and techniques can elevate your mocktails to a new level of complexity and enjoyment. For instance, you might start by muddling fresh herbs and citrus in the bottom of a shaker, then add your liquid ingredients and shake to blend and chill.

After straining the mixture into a glass, gently stir in a sparkling element to maintain its effervescence. Layering flavors in this way allows different aspects of the ingredients to shine, creating a nuanced and well-balanced drink. Textural contrasts, such as a frothily shaken top layer poured  upon a smoothly stirred base, add interest and sophistication. Timing and sequence are crucial—muddling first releases the flavors, shaking then blends and chills, and stirring at the end preserves the delicate bubbles of sparkling water or soda.

By mastering these methods, you can create a wide range of mocktails that cater to different tastes and occasions. Whether preparing a refreshing mint lemonade for a summer picnic or a sophisticated herbal tonic for an elegant dinner, these techniques will serve you well. They offer endless opportunities for creativity and experimentation, making the process of mocktail-making both fun and rewarding.

1.5 SWEETENERS: SIMPLE SYRUP, HONEY, AGAVE, AND MORE

Simple syrup is a mixture of sugar and water used in many mocktail recipes. To make your own, combine equal parts sugar and water in a saucepan over medium heat. Start with 1/2 cup of each. If you're making an infused syrup, add the spices, tea bags, or botanicals. Simmer, stirring occasionally, until the sugar dissolves.

Then, remove from heat and let the syrup cool to room temperature. Strain if needed, transfer to a clean jar or bottle, and refrigerate for up to one month.

Natural sweeteners are a healthy alternative to refined and artificial sugars. They come with added health benefits and unique flavors. Honey, for instance, is packed with antioxidants, enzymes, and minerals. It has antibacterial properties and can soothe a sore throat. Agave syrup has a mild flavor and a lower glycemic index than sugar, making it a good option for those monitoring their blood sugar levels. With its rich and complex taste, maple syrup brings a depth of flavor that pairs well with autumnal spices. Stevia and monk fruit are excellent low-calorie options. Stevia is derived from the leaves of the *Stevia* plant and is incredibly sweet, while monk fruit extract offers a natural sweetness without any calories.

Incorporating these sweeteners into your mocktails is straightforward. Dissolving honey in warm water ensures it mixes well with other ingredients. For instance, dissolve the honey in warm water before adding lemon juice and ginger when making a honey ginger lemonade. Agave syrup, on the other hand, is perfect for cold drinks as it dissolves easily without the need for heat. You can add it directly to a chilled berry spritzer for sweetness. Maple syrup's strong flavor can sometimes overpower other ingredients, so use it sparingly. It works wonderfully in spiced apple cider mocktails, adding a warm, comforting note.

Using the correct quantity of each sweetener is crucial for balancing flavors. Generally, a tablespoon of honey or agave

GETTING STARTED WITH MOCKTAILS | 21

syrup is enough to sweeten a single serving. Stevia, much sweeter than sugar, should be added drop by drop until you reach the desired sweetness. Monk fruit can also be used in small amounts, adjusting based on personal preference. This careful measurement ensures your mocktails are perfectly balanced.

You can also substitute one sweetener for another. If a fruit punch recipe calls for sugar, you can replace it with honey for a natural, more decadent sweetness. Agave syrup can replace simple syrup, offering a smooth and neutral sweetness. For those looking to cut calories, stevia is a fantastic substitute, providing sweetness without adding extra sugar. Natural sweeteners enhance the flavor of your mocktails and offer health benefits and versatility. They allow you to enjoy sweet, delicious drinks without the guilt associated with refined sugars. This flexibility will enable you to tailor mocktails to various dietary needs and preferences.

1.6 ENCOURAGING A SOBER LIFESTYLE THROUGH MOCKTAILS

Reducing or eliminating alcohol from your diet can profoundly impact your health, well-being, and social life. By replacing alcoholic drinks with mocktails, you'll likely find an increase in vitality and a more robust immune system. Sleep quality, physical stamina, and nutrient absorption will improve. Enhanced mental clarity and focus are other significant benefits. Without alcohol clouding your mind, you may experience greater emotional stability and reduced symptoms of anxiety and depression.

Social connections tend to thrive when alcohol is removed from the equation. Without its influence, relationships often become more transparent and trusting, with improved communication allowing for deeper, more meaningful interactions. Sobriety encourages healthier exchanges, free from the misunderstandings alcohol can sometimes create. Personally, my sobriety journey has helped me rediscover the true pleasure of genuine conversations and connections. At family gatherings now, I find myself appreciating the company without the fog of alcohol clouding the experience.

Beyond just creating drinks, this book is about embracing a lifestyle of well-being and connection. Mocktails can be a delightful way to promote sobriety, showing that you don't need alcohol to have a good time. Leading by example is a powerful way to encourage others. When you serve delicious, beautifully presented mocktails at your gatherings, you set a standard. People see that non-alcoholic options can be just as enjoyable, if not more so. Sharing information on the benefits of sobriety can also be enlightening. When friends and family understand the physical and mental health benefits, they are more likely to support and even join you.

For instance, at a recent family reunion, we decided to go alcohol-free. We served a range of mocktails, from simple citrus spritzers to complex herbal infusions. The feedback was overwhelmingly positive. People appreciated having delicious, non-alcoholic options, and the atmosphere was warm and welcoming.

Each chapter in this book aims to provide you with the knowledge and tools to craft mocktails that are delicious and beneficial to your health. Now that we have covered the basics, let's explore the world of seasonal mocktails. These will add timely relevance to your drink-making repertoire.

SEASONAL MOCKTAILS

Springtime brings a sense of renewal and vibrancy, making it the perfect season to explore fresh, floral, and herbal flavors in your mocktails. One of my favorite memories of spring is drinking a simple yet elegant Lavender Lemonade on my porch. The sun shone through budding trees, and the scent of blooming flowers filled the air. I took a sip, and the floral notes of lavender combined with the zesty tang of lemon. That moment helped to spark a passion for using seasonal herbs and flowers to create unique and refreshing mocktails.

2.1 SPRINGTIME FRESH: FLORAL AND HERBAL MOCKTAILS

Spring is the season of rebirth. What better way to celebrate than with mocktails that capture the essence of fresh blooms and vibrant herbs?

Lavender Lemonade is a delightful blend that combines the floral notes of lavender with the bright acidity of lemon. To make this, steep dried lavender flowers in hot water to create a lavender tea. Once it cools, mix the tea with freshly squeezed lemon juice and a touch of honey for sweetness. Serve over ice and garnish with a sprig of lavender. The result is a drink that is both refreshing and soothing, perfect for a sunny spring day. Unless otherwise noted, each recipe is per serving.

- 1 tablespoon dried lavender flowers
- 1/2 cup hot water
- 2 tablespoons lemon juice
- 1 tablespoon honey (adjust to taste)
- 1/2 cup cold water
- Ice cubes
- Fresh lavender sprigs or lemon slices for garnish

Another enchanting option is the **Rose Water Spritz**. Start by adding a splash of rose water to a glass of sparkling water. Squeeze in some fresh lemon or lime juice, and add a dash of simple syrup if you prefer a sweeter drink. The subtle floral aroma of rose water pairs beautifully with the effervescence of sparkling water, creating a light and elegant beverage.

- 1 teaspoon rose water (adjust to taste)
- 1 cup sparkling water
- 1-2 teaspoons freshly squeezed lemon or lime juice
- 1-2 teaspoons simple syrup (optional for sweetness, see Chapter 1.5)
- Ice cubes
- Rose petals or lemon/lime slices for garnish

For a more complex flavor profile, try the **Elderflower Collins**. Elderflower syrup, with its sweet and slightly fruity taste, serves as the base for this mocktail. Combine it with fresh lemon juice, mix well, add ice cubes, and top with sparkling water. Gently stir everything. Garnish with a lemon slice and a few elderflowers if available. This drink is delicious and visually stunning, making it a perfect choice for special occasions.

- 2 tablespoons elderflower syrup
- 1 tablespoon freshly squeezed lemon juice
- 1 cup sparkling water
- Ice cubes
- Lemon slices and elderflowers for garnish

A **Spring Spritzer** with strawberries and mint captures the essence of the season. Muddle fresh strawberries with mint leaves, add sparkling water, and enjoy a refreshing, light drink.

- 4-5 fresh strawberries, hulled and sliced
- 6-8 fresh mint leaves
- 1 cup sparkling water
- Ice cubes
- 1-2 teaspoons honey or agave syrup for sweetness
- Extra strawberries or mint sprigs for garnish

Using fresh, seasonal herbs adds complexity and health benefits to your mocktails. Mint, for instance, is incredibly refreshing and cooling. Its crisp, clean flavor can elevate any drink, making it a staple in spring mocktails. Basil offers a sweet and peppery note, adding depth and a touch of earthiness. With its earthy and slightly minty flavor, thyme brings a unique aromatic quality that pairs well with citrus and berries.

Spring's bounty provides an array of ingredients that can shine in your mocktails. The **Strawberry Basil Cooler** is a delightful example. Muddle fresh strawberries and basil leaves at the bottom of a glass, add ice, top with sparkling water, and gently stir. The sweetness of the strawberries combined with the peppery basil creates a balanced and refreshing drink.

- 4-5 fresh strawberries, hulled and halved
- 4-5 fresh basil leaves
- Ice cubes
- 1 cup sparkling water
- 1 teaspoon honey or agave syrup for sweetness
- Lemon or lime wedge for garnish.

Another springtime favorite is the **Cucumber Mint Refresher**. Thinly slice a cucumber and muddle it with fresh mint leaves. Fill the glass with ice and sparkling water for a hydrating and refreshing drink.

- 1/4 cucumber, thinly sliced
- 5-6 fresh mint leaves
- Ice cubes
- 1 cup sparkling water
- 1 teaspoon honey or agave syrup for sweetness
- Cucumber slice or mint sprig for garnish

For something with a bit of zing, try the **Rhubarb Ginger Fizz**. Simmer the water, rhubarb, ginger, and sugar for 10 minutes. Let it cool, and strain out the solids. Mix the syrup with sparkling water and serve over ice. Rhubarb's tartness and ginger's spiciness combine for a lively mocktail. Recipe per serving:

- 3-4 tablespoons rhubarb-infused simple syrup (see below)
- Ice cubes
- 1 cup sparkling water
- Fresh mint or lemon for garnish

Rhubarb-infused simple syrup:

- 1 cup fresh rhubarb, chopped
- 1 inch fresh ginger, peeled and sliced
- 1/2 cup water
- 1/2 cup sugar

Sourcing and storing fresh herbs and flowers can sometimes be challenging, but it's well worth the effort. Farmers' markets are excellent places to find high-quality seasonal flowers and herbs. Not only do these markets offer fresh produce, but they also support local agriculture. When you bring your herbs home, store them properly to maintain their freshness. Keep delicate herbs like mint and basil in water, much like a bouquet of flowers. Trim the stems and place them in a glass of water, then cover them loosely with a plastic bag. This method helps keep the herbs fresh for up to a week. Edible flowers can also add a beautiful and flavorful touch to your mocktails. Look for flowers that are safe to eat, such as pansies, violets, and marigolds. You can find these at farmers' markets or specialty grocers.

By embracing the vibrant flavors of spring and using fresh, seasonal ingredients, you can create delicious mocktails that reflect the season's bounty.

2.2 SUMMER HARVEST: FRUIT-FORWARD MOCKTAILS

Summer is when nature's bounty is at its peak, offering an array of vibrant and juicy fruits. Imagine sun-kissed days indulging in fresh strawberries, blueberries, and raspberries. These berries are not only delicious but also packed with antioxidants. The sweetness of strawberries, the tartness of raspberries, and the burst of blueberries can turn any mocktail into a refreshing treat. At a summer farmers' market, you can select the ripest berries, bursting with flavor, ready to be transformed into a delightful drink.

Stone fruits like peaches, plums, and cherries also make their grand entrance in summer. Juicy, succulent peaches can be paired with herbs like basil to create a harmonious blend of flavors. Plums add depth to any mocktail with their sweet and tart profile. Cherries, meanwhile, bring a touch of luxury with their rich, sweet taste. And let's not forget the melons—watermelon, cantaloupe, and honeydew are hydrating and refreshing, perfect for those scorching summer days.

Here's a recipe for a **Virgin Piña Colada** that captures the tropical flavor without the alcohol. Combine the pineapple juice, coconut cream, banana (if using), honey or agave syrup, and ice cubes. Blend until smooth and creamy. Pour into a chilled glass and garnish with a slice of pineapple and a maraschino cherry on top. Enjoy this refreshing, creamy tropical mocktail, perfect for summer!

- 1/2 cup fresh pineapple juice or blended pineapple chunks
- 1/4 cup coconut cream (coconut milk or coconut water for a lighter version)
- 1/2 ripe banana (optional for creaminess)
- 1 tablespoon honey or agave syrup
- Ice cubes
- Pineapple slices and maraschino cherries for garnish

Imagine sipping on a **Watermelon Mint Cooler**, the coolness of mint balancing the sweet, juicy watermelon, offering a moment of pure refreshment. To make this drink, blend the watermelon (strain if desired), muddle the mint, combine all ingredients, stir, and garnish.

- 1 cup fresh watermelon, cubed
- 6-8 fresh mint leaves
- 1 tablespoon lime juice
- 1-2 teaspoons honey or agave syrup
- Ice cubes
- Mint sprigs or lime wedges for garnish

One of my favorite summer mocktails is **Peach Basil Iced Tea**. Start by brewing a strong batch of your favorite tea and letting it cool. Muddle fresh peach slices with a handful of basil leaves in a pitcher. Add the cooled tea and a touch of honey, then let it chill in the fridge. Serve over ice for a drink that's both refreshing and sophisticated.

- 1 cup brewed tea (black, green, or herbal, depending on preference)
- 1 ripe peach, sliced
- 5-6 fresh basil leaves
- 1-2 tablespoons honey
- Ice cubes
- Peach slices or basil sprigs for garnish

PEACH BASIL ICED TEA

Another crowd-pleaser is the **Sparkling Berry Lemonade**. Combine freshly squeezed lemon juice with a berry puree made from a mix of your favorite summer berries. Add sparkling water for a fizzy twist, and serve over ice. The lemon's tartness perfectly complements the sweetness of the berries, making it a hit at any summer gathering.

- 1/4 cup freshly squeezed lemon juice
- 1/2 cup mixed summer berries (strawberries, raspberries, blueberries, etc.)
- 1-2 tablespoons honey or sugar
- 1/2 cup sparkling water
- Ice cubes
- Lemon slices or extra berries for garnish

For those who enjoy a bit of spice, the **Mango and Chili Fizz** is an excellent choice. This mocktail combines the sweetness of ripe mango with the subtle heat of chili, creating an exciting and refreshing drink. To prepare, blend fresh mango chunks until smooth, then mix the puree with a dash of chili powder and fresh lime juice. Pour over ice and top with sparkling water. Garnish with a slice of mango and a sprinkle of chili powder.

The sweet and spicy combination makes this drink a standout choice for summer BBQs, adding a unique twist to the usual mocktail offerings.

- 1/2 cup fresh mango chunks
- 1/4 teaspoon chili powder (adjust to taste)
- 1 tablespoon freshly squeezed lime juice
- 1/2 cup sparkling water
- Ice cubes
- Mango slice and a sprinkle of chili powder for garnish

In summer, a **Berry and Cucumber Cooler** is perfect. Combine fresh mixed berries with cucumber slices. Gently muddle them, then add sparkling water for a hydrating, flavorful mocktail.

- 1/4 cup mixed berries (such as strawberries, blueberries, and raspberries)
- 1/4 cucumber, thinly sliced
- 1 cup sparkling water
- Ice cubes
- 2 teaspoons honey or agave syrup
- Mint leaves or extra berries for garnish

Here's a simple and refreshing recipe for a **Virgin Mojito**. Muddle the mint leaves and lime wedges with the sugar in a tall glass. Press them together to release the mint's essential oils and lime juice, but don't over-muddle the mint leaves (you don't want them to become bitter). Fill the glass with ice cubes. Pour soda water and simple syrup over the ice and gently stir to combine the flavors.

Garnish with a sprig of mint and a lime wedge. Enjoy a minty and refreshing drink that is perfect for any occasion!

- 10-15 fresh mint leaves
- 2 limes cut into wedges
- 1 teaspoon raw sugar
- 1 tablespoon simple syrup (adjust to taste)
- 1 cup club soda or sparkling water
- Ice cubes
- Mint sprig and lime wedge for garnish

Proper juicing, muddling, and infusing techniques are essential to maximize the flavors of your summer fruits. When muddling fruits, use a gentle but firm hand to release the juices without pulverizing the fruit. This technique is particularly effective for softer fruits like berries and peaches. Infusing water with fruit slices is another excellent way to add subtle flavor. Simply place slices of your chosen fruit in a water pitcher and let it sit in the fridge for a few hours. This method works wonderfully with melons and citrus fruits, creating a gently flavored, hydrating drink.

Preserving the abundance of summer produce ensures you can enjoy these flavors even after the season has passed. Freezing fruit is a simple and effective method. Slice your fruits and freeze them on a tray before transferring them to a freezer bag so they don't clump together. Making fruit syrups and purees is another way to capture the essence of summer. Cook down fruits with some sugar and water to create a syrup for use in various mocktails. Purees can be made by blending fruits and then freezing them in ice cube trays, ready to be added to drinks whenever you need a burst of summer flavor.

2.3 AUTUMN FLAVORS: SPICED AND COZY MOCKTAILS

I attended a small gathering at a friend's home one crisp autumn evening. The living room was warm and inviting, filled with the aroma of spiced cider and freshly baked cookies. As we all mingled, I noticed a beautiful setup on the kitchen counter—vibrant, non-alcoholic beverages displayed in elegant glassware. My curiosity led me to a drink with its rich, ruby-red hue and sprig of rosemary. The first sip was a revelation—a burst of pomegranate, the subtle warmth of ginger, and a hint of rosemary's earthiness. It wasn't just a drink; it was an experience. That moment, surrounded by friends and feeling entirely included without a drop of alcohol, reminded me that mocktails can offer a sensory delight that surpasses their alcoholic counterparts.

Autumn brings a sense of warmth and comfort, perfect for embracing the rich, spiced flavors that define the season. Imagine a chilly evening where the air is crisp and the leaves crunch underfoot. The scent of cinnamon, nutmeg, and cloves fills the kitchen as you prepare a **Spiced Apple Cider**. Start by simmering fresh apple cider with cinnamon sticks, whole cloves, orange slices, and a dash of nutmeg for about 15 minutes. The spices infuse the cider, creating a fragrant and warming drink. Serve it hot, garnished with a cinnamon stick for an extra autumnal charm. This recipe makes about four servings.

- 4 cups fresh apple cider
- 2-3 cinnamon sticks
- 4-5 whole cloves

- 1/4 teaspoon ground nutmeg (or freshly grated)
- 1 orange, sliced
- Star anise for added spice (optional)
- Apple slices and cinnamon sticks for garnish

Another fall favorite is the **Pumpkin Spice Latte**. To make this cozy drink, combine pumpkin puree with your choice of milk, vanilla extract, and a blend of spices, including cinnamon, nutmeg, and cloves. Heat the mixture until it's warm and frothy, then sweeten to taste with a touch of maple syrup. Top with whipped cream and pumpkin spice. This mocktail is perfect for those chilly mornings when you need a comforting start to your day.

- 1 cup milk (dairy, almond, oat)
- 2 tablespoons pumpkin puree
- 1/2 teaspoon pumpkin spice mix (or a blend of ground cinnamon, nutmeg, and cloves)
- 1/4 teaspoon vanilla extract
- 1 tablespoon maple syrup (adjust to taste)

- 1/2 cup brewed coffee or shot of espresso (optional)
- Whipped cream
- Extra pumpkin spice for garnish

The **Pomegranate Ginger Fizz with Rosemary** is perfect for a refreshing burst of flavor on a fall afternoon. Combine the sliced ginger, water, and sugar in a small pot. Bring to a boil, then lower the heat and let it simmer for 10 minutes. Remove from heat, strain, and allow the syrup to cool. Muddle the rosemary sprig gently in a cocktail shaker or glass to release its flavor. Add the fresh pomegranate juice, ginger syrup, and a few ice cubes. Shake or stir well. Strain the mixture into a glass filled with ice. Top with sparkling water (or ginger beer for an extra punch). Stir gently. Garnish with pomegranate seeds and a small sprig of rosemary. Enjoy the burst of pomegranate with the warmth of ginger and rosemary's earthy finish.

- 1/2 cup fresh pomegranate juice
- 1/4 cup ginger syrup (see below)
- 1 sprig of fresh rosemary
- 1/2 cup sparkling water (or ginger beer for an extra kick)
- Ice cubes
- Pomegranate seeds and a small rosemary sprig for garnish

Ginger Syrup:

- 1/2 cup fresh ginger, peeled and sliced
- 1/2 cup water
- 1/2 cup sugar

Warm Vanilla Chai is another delightful option for cooler weather. Simmer crushed whole spices like cinnamon sticks, cardamom pods, cloves, black peppercorns, and ginger for 15 minutes. Then lower the heat and add black tea bags or loose leaves. After 5-10 minutes of steeping and melding flavors, add a splash of vanilla extract, a bit of honey for sweetness, and your choice of milk. Strain and serve hot for a creamy, spiced drink that warms you from the inside out. This recipe makes 2-3 servings.

- 2 cups water
- 1 cinnamon stick
- 4-5 cardamom pods, slightly crushed
- 4 whole cloves
- 5-6 black peppercorns
- 1 inch fresh ginger, sliced

- 2 black tea bags or 2 teaspoons of loose-leaf black tea
- 1/2 teaspoon vanilla extract
- 1-2 tablespoons honey or sweetener of choice (adjust to taste)
- 1 cup milk (any kind: dairy, almond, oat, etc.)
- Ground cinnamon for garnish

A **Spiced Pear Punch** in the fall always brings me warmth and comfort. Simmer pear slices with cinnamon sticks and cloves, then serve warm.

- 1 cup water or pear juice
- 1 pear, thinly sliced
- 1 cinnamon stick
- 2-3 whole cloves
- 1 tablespoon honey or sugar (adjust to taste)
- Star anise or fresh ginger slices for extra spice (optional)
- Apple/pear slice for garnish

Whole spices bring flavor and various health benefits to your mocktails. Infusing spices in syrups is an excellent way to incorporate their flavors. For instance, you can make a spiced simple syrup by simmering sugar, water, and whole spices like cinnamon sticks and cloves. Add this syrup to various mocktails for an extra layer of flavor. Muddling spices with fruits is another technique that releases the essential oils and enhances the overall taste of the drink. Imagine muddling fresh apple slices with cinnamon and cloves before adding them to your cider. The result is a robust, flavorful drink that captures the essence of fall.

Sourcing high-quality spices is vital to achieving the best flavors. Specialty spice shops offer fresher, more potent spices than regular grocery stores. Proper storage is crucial to maintain potency when you bring your spices home. Store whole spices in airtight containers, away from direct sunlight and heat, to preserve their essential oils and keep them fresh for extended periods. For example, cinnamon sticks and whole cloves can last up to a year if stored properly, while ground spices tend to lose their flavor more quickly.

2.4 WINTER WARMERS: COMFORTING MOCKTAIL RECIPES

Winter calls for warm, comfortable drinks, embracing rich, creamy textures and spiced, aromatic flavors. Imagine a cold evening with a warm, inviting drink that soothes the soul.

One of my favorite winter beverages is **Hot Chocolate with Peppermint**. Start by heating the milk. Whisk in cocoa powder and a bit of dark chocolate until smooth. Add a splash of peppermint extract for a refreshing twist. Serve it in an insulated mug, topped with whipped cream and a sprinkle of crushed peppermint candies. The rich, creamy texture and the cool peppermint create a comforting drink perfect for a winter night.

- 1 cup milk (dairy, almond, oat, etc.)
- 1 tablespoon cocoa powder
- 1 ounce dark chocolate, chopped
- 1 teaspoon sweetener (adjust to taste)
- 1/4 teaspoon peppermint extract
- Whipped cream
- Crushed peppermint candies for garnish

Another delightful option is **Mulled Cranberry Punch**. This drink combines cranberries' tartness with warming spices like cinnamon and cloves. Begin by simmering cranberry juice with cinnamon sticks, whole cloves, and some orange zest. Allow the spices to infuse for about 20 minutes, then strain and serve hot. Garnish with an orange slice and a cinnamon stick for an extra touch of warmth. This mocktail is delicious and visually appealing, making it an excellent choice for holiday gatherings. This recipe serves four.

- 4 cups cranberry juice (unsweetened or sweetened, depending on your preference)
- 2 cinnamon sticks
- 4-5 whole cloves
- 1 orange, zest peeled in strips
- 1-2 tablespoons honey or sweetener
- Orange slices and cinnamon sticks for garnish

In winter, a **Citrus and Pomegranate Sparkler** is very satisfying. Mix fresh citrus juices with pomegranate seeds and sparkling water for a refreshing drink. This recipe serves two.

- 1/2 cup freshly squeezed orange juice
- 3 tablespoons freshly squeezed lemon juice
- 3 tablespoons freshly squeezed lime juice

- 1/4 cup pomegranate seeds
- 1 cup sparkling water
- Ice cubes
- Mint leaves or citrus slices for garnish

For something a bit more indulgent, try a **Gingerbread Latte**. Start by making a gingerbread syrup by heating the molasses, ground ginger, cinnamon, nutmeg, and a little water, whisking until it becomes smooth and syrupy. Add the milk and heat the mixture until warm and bubbly. Add the coffee, then sweeten to taste. Top with whipped cream and a sprinkle of nutmeg for a drink that captures the essence of gingerbread cookies in a cup. This latte is perfect for a cozy morning or an afternoon pick-me-up. This recipe serves two.

- 1 cup brewed coffee or strong black tea (or 1-2 shots of espresso)
- 1 cup milk (dairy or non-dairy, such as almond or oat)
- 1 tablespoon molasses
- 1/2 teaspoon ground ginger
- 1/2 teaspoon ground cinnamon
- 1/4 teaspoon ground nutmeg
- 1-2 teaspoons sugar or sweetener (adjust to taste)
- 1/4 teaspoon vanilla extract (optional for extra flavor)
- Whipped cream for topping
- Ground nutmeg or cinnamon for garnish

Warming spices and ingredients are crucial in creating these comforting winter mocktails. Ginger adds a spicy warmth that invigorates the senses. Its ability to stimulate circulation makes it an ideal ingredient for winter drinks. Cinnamon brings a sense of nostalgia and comfort with its sweet and aromatic profile. It pairs beautifully with a variety of ingredients, adding depth and complexity. With its earthy and sweet flavor, nutmeg rounds out the spice blend, providing a subtle warmth. These spices enhance the flavor and offer health benefits like improved digestion and reduced inflammation.

Serving hot mocktails requires some preparation to ensure they remain warm and enjoyable. Insulated mugs or thermoses help retain heat, allowing you to savor the drink without cooling too quickly. When serving, consider garnishing with whipped cream and a sprinkle of spices for added visual appeal and flavor. For instance, a dollop of whipped cream on hot chocolate looks inviting and adds a creamy richness to each sip.

These winter warmers are perfect for creating a cozy atmosphere, whether hosting a gathering or simply curling up with a good book. They offer a blend of rich textures and spiced flavors that warm both the body and soul, making the cold winter months a bit more enjoyable.

2.5 FARM-TO-GLASS: SOURCING SEASONAL & LOCAL INGREDIENTS

Using seasonal ingredients offers many benefits, making your mocktails flavorful, nutritious, and sustainable. When produce is in season, it's at its peak ripeness, offering enhanced flavors that can transform your drinks. Imagine a strawberry picked at the height of spring; its sweetness and juiciness are unmatched by those grown out of season. Seasonal produce also tends to have higher nutritional value and reduced environmental impact. They require fewer resources to grow, store, and transport, making them more eco-friendly and affordable. This cost-saving aspect makes it easier to experiment with new recipes without breaking the bank.

Identifying seasonal produce can seem daunting, but it's simpler than you might think. Seasonal produce charts are a great starting point, providing a visual guide to what's in season at various times of the year. Local farmers' market guides are another valuable resource. These markets often feature the freshest in-season produce, and vendors can offer insight into what is currently at its best. Subscription services for seasonal produce boxes may also be worth considering. These services deliver a curated selection of seasonal fruits and vegetables to your doorstep, taking the guesswork out of sourcing fresh ingredients. They often include recipes and tips, making incorporating these ingredients into your mocktails easier.

The benefits of using local ingredients extend beyond just flavor. When you buy locally, you support the local economy, helping farmers sustain their livelihoods. Knowing the source of your food gives you peace of mind about its quality and safety. Local produce doesn't travel far, so it retains more nutrients and tastes better. For example, a cucumber harvested locally will be crisper and more flavorful than one shipped from hundreds of miles away. The freshness and quality of local ingredients elevate your drinks while supporting local agriculture and fostering community ties.

Spring offers strawberries, rhubarb, beets, and carrots. These ingredients bring a burst of freshness to your drinks. In summer, berries, cucumbers, watermelon, and tomatoes are abundant. Their vibrant flavors and hydrating properties make them perfect for hot-weather mocktails. Fall brings apples, pears, and pumpkins. These fruits are ideal for spiced, cozy drinks that warm you from the inside out. Winter is the season for citrus fruits, pomegranates, and root vegetables. Their robust flavors and high vitamin content are perfect for brightening the colder months.

Sourcing seasonal ingredients enhances your mocktails, supports local agriculture, and reduces your carbon footprint. By paying attention to what's in season, you can create flavorful, nutritious, and sustainable drinks. This mindful approach to ingredient selection enriches your mocktail-making experience, making each drink a true celebration of nature's bounty.

2.6 ZERO-WASTE & ECO-FRIENDLY PRACTICES IN MIXOLOGY

In a world where sustainability is becoming increasingly important, minimizing waste in the kitchen is a practical and impactful step. This concept of zero-waste is particularly relevant in mocktail making, where we can utilize every part of an ingredient to its fullest potential. Reducing food waste not only helps the environment by lowering the amount of organic waste in landfills but also maximizes the use of each ingredient, leading to cost savings. Imagine being able to create delicious mocktails while knowing that you're contributing to a more sustainable world.

When preparing your mocktails, there are several techniques to ensure that no part of your ingredients goes to waste. Zesting citrus fruits before juicing is a great start. The zest can add a burst of flavor to your drinks or be used to make flavored sugars and salts for rimming glasses. Once you've juiced the citrus, don't discard the peels. Use them as garnishes or even candied for a sweet treat. Making syrups from leftover fruit scraps is another way to use every part of your ingredients. Boil the scraps with sugar and water to create a flavorful syrup. Compost any organic waste to reduce waste and enrich your garden soil.

There are many creative ways to incorporate scraps and leftovers into new recipes. Infusing water with fruit peels is a simple yet effective method. Place the peels in a pitcher of water and let it sit in the refrigerator for a few hours to infuse. This refreshing, subtly flavored water is perfect for hydra-tion. Another fun idea is to create herbal ice cubes. Freeze leftover herbs in ice cube trays filled with water and add them to your mocktails for extra flavor. Vegetable trimmings boiled into broth create a savory base for unique mocktails. Candied fruit peels are a delicious way to recycle citrus rinds. Boil the peels in sugar syrup until they become translucent, then roll them in sugar and let them dry. These can be used as garnishes or enjoyed as sweet snacks.

Incorporating eco-friendly practices into your mocktail-making routine benefits the environment and adds a layer of mindfulness to your craft. A straightforward way to start is by using reusable straws and glassware. Reusable metal or bamboo straws are excellent alternatives to single-use plastic straws and can be easily cleaned and reused. Similarly, opting for glassware or mason jars over disposable cups reduces waste and enhances the drinking experience. Imagine serving your beautifully crafted mocktails in elegant glassware, knowing you're making a positive environmental impact.

Avoiding single-use plastics is another step towards sustainability. Instead of plastic stirrers, consider using wooden or metal ones. Bring your reusable bags to reduce plastic waste when shopping for ingredients. Choosing organic ingredients is not only better for your health but also for the environment. Organic farming practices avoid harmful pesticides and fertilizers, promoting soil health and biodiversity. When you select organic produce, you're supporting sustainable agriculture and enjoying ingredients that are richer in nutrients and flavor.

Reducing water usage is another crucial aspect of eco-friendly mixology. Be mindful of how much water you use when washing fruits and herbs. A quick rinse is often sufficient, and you can even save the rinse water for your plants. Using a pitcher to catch running water while waiting for it to heat up can also help reduce waste. These minor adjustments can make a significant difference in your overall water consumption.

Sustainable sourcing is essential for creating environmentally conscious mocktails. Opt for organic produce whenever possible, as it supports farming practices that are less environmentally harmful. Selecting fair-trade products ensures that the workers who produce your ingredients are paid fairly and work in safe conditions. In particular, coffee and chocolate come from regions with controversial labor practices. Using sustainably harvested herbs, whether from your garden or a local market, ensures you're not contributing to over-harvesting and depletion of natural resources. Avoiding over-packaged items is another way to reduce waste and support companies that prioritize sustainable packaging.

Mindful consumption habits also contribute significantly to sustainability. Only make what you need to avoid waste. Properly storing ingredients extends their shelf life, reducing the likelihood of spoilage. Educating your guests about sustainability can also make a difference. Sharing the benefits of eco-friendly practices can inspire others to adopt similar habits, creating a ripple effect of positive change.

Here are some eco-friendly mocktail recipes to get you started. For a **Garden Mint and Lime Sparkler**, muddle fresh mint leaves from your garden with lime juice, add sparkling water, and sweeten with agave syrup.

- 8-10 fresh mint leaves
- 2 tablespoons freshly squeezed lime juice (about 1 lime)
- 1-2 teaspoons agave syrup (adjust to taste)
- 1 cup sparkling water
- Ice cubes
- A mint sprig or lime wedge for garnish

Another excellent choice is a **Fair-Trade Vanilla Iced Coffee**. Brew a strong cup of fair-trade coffee, let it cool, and mix it with vanilla extract and almond milk. Serve over ice for a delicious and guilt-free caffeine boost.

- 1 cup strong brewed fair-trade coffee (cooled)
- 1/2 teaspoon vanilla extract
- 1/2 cup almond milk (or any milk of your choice)
- 1-2 teaspoons sweetener
- Ice cubes
- Whipped cream or a sprinkle of cinnamon for garnish

A **Zero-Waste Citrus Honey Infusion** makes use of every part of the fruit. Simmer citrus peels in water to extract their flavor, add a bit of honey, stir until dissolved, then strain, let cool, and serve over ice. This drink is flavorful and minimizes waste, aligning perfectly with sustainable practices.

- Peels from 2-3 citrus fruits (lemons, oranges, limes, or a mix)
- 2 cups water
- 2-3 tablespoons honey (adjust to taste)

- Ice cubes
- Citrus slices or mint leaves for garnish

Finally, a **Veggie and Spice Cooler** can use vegetable trimmings like cucumber and carrot peels. Muddle the trimmings with spices like cinnamon and cloves, then add water and let it sit in the fridge for 2-4 hours or overnight. Strain and serve over ice for a unique and refreshing mocktail. This recipe makes four servings.

- 1 cup veggie peels (cucumber, carrot, etc)
- 1 cinnamon stick
- 3-4 whole cloves
- 4 cups water
- Ice cubes
- Mint leaves or thin slices of cucumber or carrot for garnish

By incorporating these practices into your routine, you contribute to a more sustainable world while enjoying delicious and mindful drinks. As you explore these practices, you'll find that making environmentally conscious choices becomes second nature, enriching your mixology experience.

MOCKTAILS FOR SOCIAL GATHERINGS

Imagine a sophisticated evening gathering, where the clinking of crystal glasses and soft murmurs of conversation fill the room. The atmosphere is elegant, the lighting is dim, and fresh aromas fill the air. At the center of this scene is a beautifully crafted mocktail, its layers of flavor inviting each guest to take a moment and savor the experience.

3.1 SOPHISTICATED SIPPERS

Creating elegant and complex mocktails for adult guests is an art that combines layered flavors, unique ingredients, and upscale presentation. The appeal lies in the ability to craft a drink that engages the senses, offering a depth of flavor and a visual feast. Think of a mocktail where the initial sip reveals the delicate notes of Earl Grey tea, followed by the subtle floral hint of lavender, and all garnished with a lemon twist. This complexity makes each sip an exploration, inviting guests to appreciate the intricate balance of flavors.

To prepare this **Earl Grey and Lavender Tonic**, brew a strong cup of Earl Grey tea and let it cool. Add a simple lavender syrup made by simmering lavender flowers in water and sugar. Strain out the flowers, mix the tea and syrup, then top it with tonic water. Serve it in a crystal glass with a sprig of lavender and a lemon twist for a touch of elegance. Combining robust tea and floral lavender creates a sophisticated and intriguing drink.

- 1 cup strong brewed Earl Grey tea
- 2 tablespoons lavender simple syrup (see Chapter 1.5)
- 1/2 cup tonic water
- Ice cubes
- Sprig of lavender and lemon twist for garnish

Another refined option is the **Cucumber and Elderflower Fizz**. Start by muddling fresh cucumber slices in a shaker. Add elderflower syrup and fresh lime juice, then shake well with ice. Strain the mixture into a highball glass and top it with sparkling water. Garnish with a cucumber ribbon and a sprig of mint. This mocktail offers a crisp, clean flavor profile, with elderflower adding a sweet, floral note that complements the freshness of cucumber.

- 4-5 cucumber slices
- 2 tablespoons elderflower syrup
- 2 tablespoons freshly squeezed lime juice
- 1 cup sparkling water

MOCKTAILS FOR SOCIAL GATHERINGS | 51

- Ice cubes
- Cucumber ribbon and mint sprig for garnish

Try the **Hibiscus and Pomegranate Cooler** for a visually stunning and complex drink. Brew a strong hibiscus tea and let it cool. Mix it with pomegranate juice and a splash of lime. Serve it over ice in a tall glass garnished with pomegranate seeds and a mint sprig. The tartness of the hibiscus pairs beautifully with the sweetness of the pomegranate, creating a balanced and refreshing mocktail.

- 1 cup brewed hibiscus tea (cooled)
- 1/2 cup pomegranate juice
- 1 tablespoon freshly squeezed lime juice
- Ice cubes
- Pomegranate seeds and mint sprig for garnish

This **Citrus Rosemary Sparkler** offers a delicate balance of sweet, tart, and herbal notes—perfect for impressing guests with a refined, non-alcoholic option at your dinner party. In a small saucepan, gently heat the honey with the sprig of rosemary for about 5 minutes to infuse the rosemary flavor. Remove from heat and let cool slightly. Discard the rosemary sprig. In a shaker, combine the fresh grapefruit juice, lemon juice, rosemary-infused honey, and orange blossom water (if using). Stir or shake well to blend. Fill glasses with ice and pour the citrus mixture over the ice. Top with sparkling water or club soda for a refreshing fizz. Garnish each glass with a slice of grapefruit and a small sprig of fresh rosemary to add a touch of elegance. This recipe makes two servings.

- 1 cup fresh grapefruit juice
- 1/2 cup fresh lemon juice
- 2 tablespoons honey (or agave syrup for a vegan option)
- 1 sprig of fresh rosemary (plus extra for garnish)
- 1/2 teaspoon orange blossom water (optional for extra sophistication)
- 1 cup sparkling water or club soda
- Ice cubes
- Grapefruit slices for garnish

Consider using premium ingredients to enhance the sophistication of these drinks. High-quality teas, organic herbs, and fresh, locally sourced fruits can enhance the experience. Adding edible gold flakes to the garnish can provide a touch of luxury, making each drink feel special. Presentation is vital—serve these mocktails in crystal glasses to enhance their visual appeal. The clarity and sparkle of the glassware can make the colors of the drink pop, adding to the overall aesthetic.

Pairing these sophisticated sippers with the right appetizers can create a complete and satisfying experience for your guests. Consider a cheese platter with various cheeses, fruits, and nuts. The cheese's richness can complement the mocktails' complexity, creating a harmonious balance of flavors. Stuffed mushrooms are another excellent choice. Their earthy flavor and creamy texture can provide a delightful contrast to the crispness of the drinks.

By thoughtfully crafting sophisticated beverages, you create an environment where guests feel valued and indulged, elevating your gathering to a memorable event. The art of mocktail-making is not just about mixing ingredients; it's about creating an experience that delights the senses and brings people together in celebration.

3.2 LARGE BATCH MOCKTAILS FOR PARTIES

Imagine hosting a lively summer gathering where guests mingle, laugh, and enjoy the refreshing drinks you've prepared. Large-batch mocktails are a perfect fit for such occasions. They offer convenience for you as the host, allowing you to prepare a substantial quantity in advance, ensuring consistent flavor throughout the event. This approach means you won't be tied to the kitchen, making individual drinks, but rather enjoying the party alongside your guests. Large-batch mocktails also have the advantage of serving many guests quickly, ensuring that no one is left waiting for a drink.

Each recipe makes approximately four servings, depending on the size of the glasses and how much ice you use. You can quickly multiply the quantities to match your needs!

One fantastic large-batch mocktail recipe is the **Citrus Punch with Mint**. Combine freshly squeezed orange, lemon, and lime juices in a large pitcher. Add a generous handful of fresh mint leaves and a touch of honey for sweetness. Let the mixture sit in the refrigerator for a few hours to allow the flavors to meld. Just before serving, add sparkling water and ice. This punch is vibrant and zesty, perfect for a hot summer day. The mint's coolness balances its bright citrus notes, creating a flavorful and invigorating drink.

- 1 cup freshly squeezed orange juice
- 1/4 cup freshly squeezed lemon juice
- 1/4 cup freshly squeezed lime juice
- 1-2 tablespoons honey (adjust to taste)

- 10-12 fresh mint leaves
- 3 cups sparkling water
- Ice cubes
- Extra citrus slices and mint sprigs for garnish

The **Berry and Basil Sangria** is another crowd-pleaser. Start with a base of mixed berry juice, such as blueberry, raspberry, and strawberry. Add fresh basil leaves and a splash of lime juice. For an added layer of complexity, include sliced fresh berries and a bit of agave syrup. Let the mixture chill in a large dispenser for several hours. Before serving, top it with sparkling water and ice. This mocktail offers a delightful combination of sweet berries and aromatic basil, making it a sophisticated yet approachable option for any gathering.

- 3 cups mixed berry juice (blueberry, raspberry, strawberry)
- 1/2 cup freshly squeezed lime juice
- 10-15 fresh basil leaves
- 1 cup mixed fresh berries (blueberries, raspberries, strawberries)
- 2-3 tablespoons agave syrup (adjust to taste)
- 1 cup sparkling water
- Ice cubes
- Extra berries and basil leaves for garnish

For a tropical twist, try the **Tropical Pineapple and Coconut Cooler**. Mix pineapple juice, coconut water, and a splash of lime juice in a large punch bowl. Add slices of fresh pineapple and a handful of mint leaves. Let it chill in the refrigerator, and just

MOCKTAILS FOR SOCIAL GATHERINGS | 55

before serving, stir in some crushed ice. This cooler transports you to a tropical paradise with its sweet and tangy flavors, complemented by the refreshing taste of coconut water. It's a perfect drink for a beach-themed party or a backyard barbecue.

- 2 cups pineapple juice
- 2 cups coconut water
- 1/4 cup freshly squeezed lime juice
- 6-8 slices of fresh pineapple
- 10-15 fresh mint leaves
- Ice (crushed or cubes)
- Extra pineapple slices and mint sprigs for garnish

Preparation is critical when it comes to large-batch mocktails. Start by preparing your ingredients ahead of time. Squeeze the citrus fruits, slice the berries, and muddle the herbs well before the party starts. Using large dispensers or punch bowls makes serving easy and adds to the visual appeal. Keep the mocktails chilled by adding ice just before serving or placing the dispensers in a bucket of ice to ensure that your drinks stay cool and refreshing throughout the event.

Consider garnishing your large batch mocktails with fresh fruit slices or herb sprigs to enhance the flavor and make the drinks visually attractive. Using decorative punch bowls can add a touch of elegance to your setup. Provide ladles and cups for self-service, allowing guests to help themselves. This setup makes it easier for you as the host and creates a relaxed and inviting atmosphere where guests feel comfortable.

Imagine a summer garden party where a large glass dispenser filled with Citrus Punch with Mint takes center stage. The bright colors of the citrus fruits and the green mint leaves catch the eye, inviting guests to fill their glasses. Nearby, a punch bowl brimming with Tropical Pineapple and Coconut Cooler, garnished with pineapple slices and mint sprigs, adds a tropical flair. Guests gather around, chatting and laughing, holding beautifully garnished glasses.

Creating large batch mocktails for parties is a thoughtful way to ensure all your guests have a delightful and consistent experience. These drinks are not just about quenching thirst; they create an atmosphere of enjoyment and relaxation, making your gathering memorable for everyone.

3.3 ELEGANT BRUNCH MOCKTAILS

Brunch is a pleasant time that blends the best of breakfast and lunch, creating a relaxed yet sophisticated atmosphere perfect for enjoying elegant mocktails. These drinks should be light and refreshing, complementing the flavors of classic brunch dishes. Imagine a table set with avocado toast, banana pancakes, and fresh fruit salad, each dish enhanced by a thoughtfully crafted mocktail. The right drink can add a touch of sophistication to your brunch, making it an event to remember.

One terrific brunch mocktail is the **Sparkling Peach and Thyme Spritzer**. This drink combines the sweet, juicy flavor of ripe peaches with the subtle earthiness of fresh thyme. Puree fresh peaches and strain to remove any pulp. Mix the peach puree with a thyme-infused simple syrup and top with sparkling water. Serve it in a champagne flute, garnished with a sprig of thyme and a thin slice of peach. This spritzer is light, bubbly, and perfect for pairing with savory dishes like avocado toast. The peach's sweetness balances the avocado's richness, while the thyme adds a sophisticated herbal note.

- 1 ripe peach, peeled and chopped
- 2 tablespoons thyme-infused simple syrup (See Chapter 1.5)
- 1 cup sparkling water
- Ice cubes
- Peach slices for garnish

Here's a simple recipe for a **Shirley Temple**, perfect for family brunch. Fill a glass with ice cubes, pour the grenadine syrup over the ice, then pour in the ginger ale (or soda). If using orange juice, add it here for a twist on the classic. Stir gently, then garnish with maraschino cherries and orange or lemon slices.

- 1/2 cup ginger ale (or lemon-lime soda)
- 1/4 cup orange juice (optional for an extra twist)
- 2 tablespoons grenadine syrup (see recipe below)
- Ice cubes
- Maraschino cherries for garnish
- Orange or lemon slices for garnish

Here's a simple recipe to make **Homemade Grenadine Syrup**. In a small saucepan, combine the pomegranate juice and sugar. Place the saucepan over medium heat and stir until the sugar completely dissolves. Do not let the mixture boil. You just want to warm it enough to dissolve the sugar. Once the sugar dissolves, stir in the lemon juice for a slight tartness. Add a few drops of orange blossom water for a subtle floral note if desired. Remove the syrup from heat and allow it to cool completely. Once cool, transfer the grenadine syrup to a clean bottle or jar and store it in the refrigerator.

- 1 cup pomegranate juice (fresh or store-bought)
- 1 cup granulated sugar
- 1 tablespoon lemon juice
- 1-2 drops of orange blossom water (optional for added aroma)

Another excellent choice is the **Grapefruit and Rosemary Cooler.** This mocktail offers a refreshing burst of citrus with a hint of aromatic rosemary. Start by juicing fresh grapefruits and mixing the juice with a rosemary-infused syrup. Add a splash of lime juice for extra brightness. Serve over ice in a highball glass garnished with a rosemary sprig and a slice of grapefruit. This drink pairs beautifully with banana pancakes, as the citrus cuts through the richness while the rosemary adds a unique twist that elevates the overall flavor.

- 2 cups fresh grapefruit juice
- 1/4 cup freshly squeezed lime juice
- 4 tablespoons rosemary-infused syrup (See Chapter 1.5)
- Ice cubes
- Grapefruit slices and rosemary sprigs for garnish

For a more exotic option, consider the **Coconut Mango Lassi.** Traditional lassi is a creamy, yogurt-based drink from India, but this version adds a modern spin. Blend fresh mango chunks with Greek yogurt, a splash of coconut milk, and a touch of honey. Add a pinch of cardamom for an aromatic depth. Serve chilled in a tall glass, garnished with a sprinkle of crushed pistachios and a mint leaf. This rich and creamy lassi makes it a perfect match for a fresh fruit salad. The tropical flavors of the mango and coconut complement the natural sweetness of the fruit, while the yogurt adds a tangy, refreshing note.

- 1 cup fresh mango chunks
- 1/2 cup Greek yogurt
- 1/2 cup coconut milk
- 1-2 tablespoons honey (adjust to taste)
- 1/4 teaspoon ground cardamom
- Ice cubes (optional for a chilled lassi)
- Crushed pistachios and mint leaves for garnish

Preparation is essential to ensure these brunch mocktails are fresh and delicious. Start by preparing your ingredients the night before. Juice the fruits, make the syrups, and puree any necessary ingredients in advance so you can focus on assembling the drinks without rushing. Chilling your glasses ahead of time can make a big difference, keeping your mocktails cold and refreshing for longer. Add your garnishes just before serving to ensure they are fresh and vibrant. A sprig of mint, a slice of fruit, or a delicate herb garnish can make your drinks look as good as they taste.

Elegant brunch mocktails bring a touch of sophistication to your mid-morning gatherings. They offer a delightful way to enhance the flavors of your brunch dishes, making the meal more enjoyable and memorable. Whether hosting a casual get-together with friends or a more formal brunch, these mocktails provide the perfect finishing touch, turning an ordinary meal into a special occasion.

3.4 MOCKTAILS FOR DINNER PARTIES

Dinner parties offer a unique opportunity to impress your guests with sophisticated and complementary mocktails. These carefully crafted beverages can enhance the dining experience, providing a harmonious balance with each course of the meal. Imagine welcoming your guests with a beautifully presented mocktail that refreshes and sets the tone for an elegant evening. The right mocktail can elevate your dinner party, making it a memorable event for everyone involved.

One of my favorite dinner party mocktails is the **Rosemary and Lemon Spritz.** This drink combines the earthy aroma of rosemary with the bright, zesty flavor of lemon. To make it, start by infusing a simple syrup with fresh rosemary. Mix this syrup with freshly squeezed lemon juice and sparkling water. Serve in a tall glass with a sprig of rosemary and a lemon wheel for garnish. This spritz is light and refreshing, perfect for pairing with appetizers. The rosemary's herbal notes and the lemon's citrusy brightness make it an excellent match for light, savory bites like bruschetta or a crisp salad.

- 1/2 cup freshly squeezed lemon juice
- 4 tablespoons rosemary-infused syrup (see Chapter 1.5)
- 1 cup sparkling water

MOCKTAILS FOR SOCIAL GATHERINGS | 61

- Ice cubes
- Lemon wheels and rosemary sprigs for garnish

The **Blueberry and Basil Cooler** is another elegant option for a dinner party. This mocktail offers a charming combination of sweet blueberries and aromatic basil. Begin by muddling fresh blueberries and basil leaves in a shaker. Add a splash of lime juice and a bit of honey for sweetness. Shake well with ice and strain into a highball glass. Top with sparkling water and garnish with a few whole blueberries and a basil leaf. This drink's complexity and balance make it an excellent choice for the main course, especially complementing rich, savory flavors like grilled vegetables or hearty pasta.

- 1/2 cup fresh blueberries
- 6-8 fresh basil leaves
- 2 tablespoons freshly squeezed lime juice
- 1 tablespoon honey (adjust to taste)
- Ice cubes
- 1 cup sparkling water
- Basil leaf and whole blueberries for garnish

The **Ginger and Pear Fizz** is an excellent choice for those looking to add warmth to their dinner party. This mocktail pairs the spicy kick of ginger with the subtle sweetness of pear. To create it, start by juicing fresh ginger and pears. Mix the juices with a touch of honey and a splash of lime. Serve over ice in a rocks glass, topped with club soda. Garnish with a thin slice of pear and a twist of lime. The warming ginger and sweet pear complement robust main courses like roasted root vegetables or a spiced lentil stew.

- 1 tablespoon ginger juice
- 1/2 cup fresh pear juice
- 1 tablespoon honey (adjust to taste)
- 2 tablespoons freshly squeezed lime juice
- Ice cubes
- 1/2 cup club soda
- Thin pear slices and lime twist for garnish

Coordinating these mocktails with different courses enhances the overall dining experience. Light and refreshing drinks like the Rosemary and Lemon Spritz are ideal for pairing with appetizers. They cleanse the palate and prepare guests for the meal ahead. More robust flavors, such as those in the Blueberry and Basil Cooler, work well with the main course, balancing the richness of the food. Offering a palate cleanser between courses can also elevate the dining experience.

A small serving of a simple mocktail, like a **Citrus Sorbet Float**, can refresh the palate and prepare guests for the next dish. Place 1-2 scoops of citrus sorbet in a tall glass. Pour the freshly squeezed lemon or lime juice over the sorbet for an extra burst of tartness. Slowly pour the sparkling water or club soda over the sorbet, letting it fizz and combine. Garnish with fresh mint leaves or a citrus slice for a decorative touch.

- 1-2 scoops of citrus sorbet (lemon, lime, or orange)
- 1 cup sparkling water or club soda
- 1 tablespoon freshly squeezed lemon or lime juice
- Fresh mint leaves or citrus slices for garnish

Presentation plays a crucial role in serving dinner party mocktails. Using elegant stemware can add a touch of sophistication to your drinks. Consider serving the Rosemary and Lemon Spritz in a champagne flute, the Blueberry and Basil Cooler in a highball glass, and the Ginger and Pear Fizz in a rocks glass. Adding sophisticated garnishes, such as a sprig of rosemary, a basil leaf, or a twist of lime, enhances the visual appeal of the drinks. Serving the mocktails on a tray with napkins can also add an element of formality to the presentation, making your guests feel pampered and special.

Imagine a dinner party where each course pairs with a complementary mocktail. Guests start with a Rosemary and Lemon Spritz, enjoying its refreshing notes alongside light appetizers. With the main course, they switch to a Blueberry and Basil Cooler, its complexity balancing the meal's richness. Between courses, a small citrus sorbet float cleanses the palate, preparing them for the next dish. Finally, the evening concludes with a Ginger and Pear Fizz, its warming flavors offering a satisfying end to the meal. This thoughtful pairing of mocktails with each course enhances the flavors of the food and creates a cohesive and memorable dining experience.

3.5 QUICK AND EASY MOCKTAILS FOR LAST-MINUTE GUESTS

There's nothing quite like the surprise of last-minute guests knocking at your door, eager to catch up or celebrate spontaneously. Having a few go-to mocktails to prepare quickly is helpful in these moments. Such drinks should require minimal ingredients and simple preparation, delivering fast and delicious results. Whether it's an impromptu family gathering, an unexpected visit from friends, or a sudden craving for a refreshing drink, these mocktails ensure you're always ready to entertain with style and ease.

One quick and delightful mocktail is the **Lemon and Mint Spritzer**. This drink is incredibly refreshing and takes just a few minutes to prepare. Start by squeezing the juice of a fresh lemon into a glass. Add a handful of torn mint leaves and a spoonful of honey. Fill the glass with ice and top it off with sparkling water. Give it a gentle stir, and garnish with a lemon slice and a sprig of mint. The result is a light, zesty drink perfect for any impromptu gathering.

- 2 tablespoons fresh lemon juice
- 6-8 fresh mint leaves, torn
- 1-2 teaspoons honey (adjust to taste)
- Ice cubes
- 1 cup sparkling water
- Lemon slice and mint sprig for garnish

Another fantastic option is the **Orange and Ginger Sparkler**. This mocktail combines orange juice's bright sweetness with ginger's warming spice. To make it, pour freshly squeezed orange juice into a glass. Add a dash of ginger syrup or freshly grated ginger for some heat. Fill the glass with ice and top it with club soda. Stir gently, and garnish with an orange wheel and a piece of candied ginger. This drink is quick to make and offers a delightful balance of flavors that can impress any guest.

- 1 cup freshly squeezed orange juice
- 1 tablespoon ginger-infused syrup (See Chapter 1.5) or freshly grated ginger

- Ice cubes
- 1/2 cup club soda
- Orange wheel and candied ginger for garnish

For a festive and tart option, try the **Cranberry and Lime Refresher**. This mocktail is perfect for those who enjoy a bit of tanginess in their drinks. Start by mixing cranberry and lime juices in a glass. Add a splash of simple syrup to balance the tartness. Fill the glass with ice and top it with sparkling water. Stir gently, and garnish with a few cranberries and a lime wheel. This drink is as visually appealing as it is tasty, making it an excellent choice for any sudden celebration.

- 1 cup cranberry juice
- 2 tablespoons fresh lime juice
- 1 tablespoon simple syrup (See Chapter 1.5)
- Ice cubes
- 1/2 cup sparkling water
- Fresh cranberries and lime wheel for garnish

Preparation is vital to ensuring these mocktails come together quickly and efficiently. Keep ingredients like lemons, limes, oranges, mint, honey, and ginger on hand. Use these versatile ingredients in various combinations to create a range of drinks. Pre-chilled beverages can save precious minutes, so keep a few bottles of sparkling water or club soda in the fridge. Simplifying garnishes is also essential. Use easy-to-prep items like citrus slices, mint sprigs, or a handful of berries to add elegance without wasting too much time. A colorful garnish can make a big difference.

Even with limited time, you can make these mocktails look impressive with a few presentation hacks. Use attractive glassware that elevates the drink's appearance. A simple highball glass or a mason jar can add a rustic charm, while a sleek tumbler offers a modern touch. Another trick is using ice molds to create large, slow-melting ice cubes that keep drinks cold and look sophisticated.

Imagine a scenario where friends drop by unexpectedly on a warm summer afternoon. You whip up a batch of Lemon and Mint Spritzers in minutes, serving them in chilled glasses, each garnished with a lemon slice and a mint sprig. Your friends are delighted, not just by the refreshing taste but also by the thoughtful presentation. This ease and efficiency make hosting last-minute guests a breeze, ensuring you can enjoy their company without stress.

Having a repertoire of quick and easy mocktails means you're always prepared to offer hospitality at a moment's notice. These drinks balance simplicity and flavor perfectly, allowing you to entertain effortlessly. With these recipes, you can consistently offer something special to your guests.

MAKE A DIFFERENCE WITH YOUR REVIEW

UNLOCK THE POWER OF GENEROSITY

"We rise by lifting others."

— ROBERT INGERSOLL

My mission is to help everyone whip up fun, flavorful, and healthy drinks with ease. That's precisely what *Mocktails Made Easy* is all about.

But here's the thing—most people pick up a book based on reviews. And that's where you come in! If you enjoy this book, would you take a moment to help someone else on their mocktail-making journey?

Small, kind acts can make a significant difference in someone's life. When we share a little bit of ourselves, like by writing a review, we can encourage someone else to make a positive decision.

Your review could help:

- One more host create a memorable gathering for friends and family.
- One more person enjoy a refreshing drink without the alcohol.
- One more parent create fun, family-friendly beverages for their kids.
- One more celebration be filled with tasty, alcohol-free drinks.

It doesn't cost a thing, and it only takes a minute—but your words could make a real difference.

Thank you for being someone who loves to help others. You're truly appreciated!

Warmly,

- Eric Santagada

Scan the QR code below

MOCKTAILS FOR SPECIAL OCCASIONS

During one particularly festive Thanksgiving, I was in the kitchen, preparing a feast for friends and family. As I stirred the pot of simmering spiced apple cider, the aroma of cinnamon and cloves filled the air, creating an atmosphere of warmth and celebration. That moment, surrounded by loved ones and the comforting scents of the season, helped me realize the power of holiday-themed drinks. They don't just quench thirst; they enhance the festive spirit, creating memorable experiences that linger long after the last sip.

4.1 HOLIDAY-THEMED MOCKTAILS

Creating special holiday drinks can elevate the festive atmosphere, turning a simple gathering into a memorable celebration. Themed drinks cater to each holiday's specific flavors and traditions, making the occasion unique and special.

Imagine the joy of festive glasses filled with a **Christmas Cranberry and Rosemary Spritzer**, the tartness balanced by rosemary's aromatic touch. This drink not only tastes like the holidays but also looks the part, with its deep red hue and green garnish evoking the colors of Christmas.

Muddle the fresh cranberries and rosemary sprigs in a large glass or pitcher. Add cranberry juice and lemon or lime juice for a tart kick. Add honey or agave syrup if you want a touch of sweetness, and stir well to combine. Just before serving, top the mixture with sparkling water or club soda. Fill glasses with ice cubes and pour the cranberry-rosemary mix over the ice. Garnish with a few fresh cranberries and a sprig of rosemary for a festive touch. This recipe serves two.

- 1 cup cranberry juice (unsweetened for a more tart flavor, or sweetened)
- 1/4 cup fresh cranberries (plus extra for garnish)
- 2-3 fresh rosemary sprigs (plus extra for garnish)
- 1 tablespoon freshly squeezed lemon or lime juice
- 1-2 teaspoons honey or agave syrup
- 1 cup sparkling water or club soda
- Ice cubes
- Fresh cranberries and rosemary sprigs for garnish

For Thanksgiving, a **Spiced Apple Cider** can be the star of the show. See Chapter 2.3 for our recipe. The combination of apple cider, cinnamon sticks, cloves, and a hint of nutmeg creates a warm, comforting drink that pairs perfectly with a bountiful dinner. As the cider simmers on the stove, the entire house fills with the inviting scents of the season, making everyone feel at

MOCKTAILS FOR SPECIAL OCCASIONS | 71

home. Serve it in a large, clear pitcher, allowing guests to see the beautiful blend of spices and apple slices.

Halloween calls for something more playful yet still fitting the autumnal theme. Enter the **Pumpkin Spice Cooler.** Blend pumpkin puree, cinnamon, nutmeg, and ginger with a splash of apple juice. Mix with soda water and serve in a spooky glass with a cinnamon stick for stirring. It pairs wonderfully with Halloween treats like caramel apples and pumpkin cookies, adding a fun and festive touch to the celebration.

- 1/2 cup pumpkin puree
- 1/2 cup apple juice
- 1/8 teaspoon ground cinnamon
- 1/8 teaspoon ground nutmeg
- 1/8 teaspoon ground ginger
- 1 tablespoon maple syrup or honey
- 1 cup soda water or sparkling water
- Ice cubes
- Cinnamon stick for stirring, ground cinnamon for garnish

Easter brings the promise of spring, and what better way to celebrate than with a **Lemon and Lavender Fizz**? This mocktail is a refreshing blend of fresh lemon juice, lavender syrup, and sparkling water. The light, floral notes of lavender complement the lemon's tartness, creating a refreshing and elegant drink. Serve it in pastel-colored glassware garnished with a lemon wheel and a sprig of lavender. This drink is perfect for an Easter brunch, pairing beautifully with vegan quiche, fresh fruit salad, and hot cross buns. To make the syrup, simmer lavender flowers in water and sugar, then strain out the flowers (see Chapter 1.5).

- 1/2 cup freshly squeezed lemon juice
- 3 tablespoons lavender syrup
- 1 cup sparkling water
- Ice cubes
- Lemon wheels and fresh lavender sprigs for garnish

Presentation plays a crucial role in enhancing the holiday theme of these mocktails. Using holiday-themed glassware can add a festive touch. For Christmas, consider using glasses adorned with snowflakes or holly. Thanksgiving mocktails can be served in rustic mason jars, giving a cozy, homey feel. Halloween drinks might look spookier in dark, gothic-style glasses, while Easter mocktails can shine in delicate, pastel-colored goblets. Adding festive garnishes further elevates the presentation. A sprig of rosemary, a cinnamon stick, or a slice of citrus can transform a simple drink into a festive masterpiece. Incorporating seasonal colors, like the reds and greens of Christmas or the yellows and purples of Easter, can make your mocktails visually appealing and on-theme.

Holiday mocktails also pair wonderfully with traditional holiday foods, enhancing the overall dining experience. The Christmas Cranberry and Rosemary Spritzer complements the sweetness of Christmas cookies, creating a pleasurable balance of flavors. Thanksgiving Spiced Apple Cider is a perfect match for tofurky and stuffing, its warm spices harmonizing with the savory elements of the meal. The Pumpkin Spice Cooler pairs well with Halloween treats, its rich, spicy flavors echoing the autumnal goodness of pumpkin and cinnamon. The Lemon and Lavender Fizz provides a refreshing contrast to the rich, savory dishes of an Easter brunch, its light and floral notes cleansing the palate between bites.

Incorporating holiday-themed mocktails into your celebrations can transform any gathering into a memorable event. These drinks taste delicious and capture the season's essence, making guests feel special. Whether hosting a large family gathering or an intimate dinner party, these mocktails add a touch of elegance and festivity that everyone can enjoy. So, as you prepare for your next holiday celebration, consider adding these themed mocktails to your menu. They will surely delight your guests and make your holiday gatherings even more special.

4.2 BIRTHDAY BASH MOCKTAILS

Birthdays are special occasions that deserve a touch of festivity and excitement, and what better way to add flair than with custom mocktails? These drinks can be tailored to the birthday person's preferences, adding a personal touch that makes the celebration even more memorable. Customizing drinks for the birthday person shows thoughtfulness and adds a layer of fun and festivity. These mocktails' vibrant colors and unique flavors create a celebratory atmosphere that everyone can enjoy, making a birthday bash unforgettable.

One delightful recipe to consider is the **Birthday Cake Batter Shake**. This mocktail captures the essence of a birthday cake in a drinkable form. Start by blending vanilla ice cream with a splash of milk, a dash of vanilla extract, and a small piece of birthday cake. Pour the mixture into a glass and top it with whipped cream, colorful sprinkles, and a cherry. The result is a rich, creamy shake that tastes like a slice of birthday cake, perfect for kids and adults with a sweet tooth.

- 2 scoops vanilla ice cream
- 1/2 cup milk (any kind)
- 1/2 teaspoon vanilla extract
- 1 small slice of birthday cake (about 2-3 tablespoons of cake)
- Whipped cream for topping
- Colorful sprinkles and maraschino cherry for garnish

For a burst of color and flavor, the **Rainbow Fruit Punch** is a fantastic option. This mocktail combines a variety of fruit juices to create a layered, rainbow-colored drink. Begin with a base of cranberry juice, then fill the glass with ice (this helps prevent mixing). Carefully pour each layer of juice over the back of a spoon to keep the colors separate. Garnish with a skewer of fresh fruit and a colorful paper straw. This drink is visually stunning and packed with a medley of fruity flavors that will delight guests of all ages.

- 1/2 cup cranberry juice
- 1/2 cup orange juice
- 1/2 cup pineapple juice
- 1/2 cup blueberry juice
- Ice cubes
- Fresh fruit skewers (strawberries, orange slices, pineapple chunks, blueberries) for garnish
- Colorful paper straw

Another favorite is the **Sparkling Strawberry Lemonade**. Make this refreshing mocktail by blending fresh strawberries, lemon juice, and a touch of honey into a purée. Pour the mixture over ice and top with sparkling water. Garnish with a lemon wheel and a fresh strawberry. The combination of sweet strawberries and tart lemon creates a balanced celebratory drink, making it an excellent choice for a summer birthday party.

- 1/2 cup fresh strawberries, hulled and sliced
- 1/2 cup freshly squeezed lemon juice
- 2-3 tablespoons honey (adjust to taste)
- 1 cup sparkling water
- Ice cubes
- Lemon wheels and fresh strawberries for garnish

For chocolate lovers, the **Chocolate-Covered Cherry Cooler** is a must-try. This mocktail starts with a base of cherry juice and chocolate syrup. Shake the ingredients with ice and strain them into a glass. Top with soda water and garnish with a chocolate-dipped cherry. The rich chocolate and sweet cherry flavors complement each other beautifully, creating a decadent drink that feels like a special treat.

- 1 cup cherry juice
- 2 tablespoons chocolate syrup
- 1/2 cup soda water
- Ice cubes
- Chocolate-dipped cherries for garnish

To make birthdays even more unique, consider adding personalized drink toppers. These can be anything from the birthday person's name to fun shapes that match the party theme. Using colorful and edible glitter can also add a magical touch to the mocktails, making them sparkle and shine.

Interactive mocktail ideas can make the celebration even more engaging. A DIY mocktail bar setup is a fantastic way to get guests involved. Provide a variety of juices, syrups, sparkling water, and a selection of fresh fruits and herbs. Offer a range of mix-ins like flavored syrups, honey, agave, and toppings like whipped cream, sprinkles, and fruit slices. Supply recipe cards with different mocktail combinations for inspiration or encourage guests to create their own. This setup allows guests to experiment with flavors and customize their drinks to their liking, adding an element of creativity and personalization to the celebration.

Another interactive idea is to host a mocktail-making contest, where guests can compete to create the best birthday mocktail. Provide a range of ingredients and tools, and let the creativity flow. To add an element of competition, you can even award prizes for the most colorful, creative, and best-tasting mocktails.

Incorporating these ideas into your birthday celebrations can transform a simple gathering into a fun and festive event. The custom mocktails, personalized touches, and interactive elements create a lively and engaging atmosphere that guests will remember long after the party. Whether you're hosting a birthday bash for a child, a teenager, or an adult, these mocktail ideas add a special touch that makes the celebration unique and memorable. So, consider adding these delightful mocktails to your menu as you plan your next birthday celebration. They will bring joy, laughter, and magic to the special day.

4.3 WEDDING AND BABY SHOWER MOCKTAILS

Envision a wedding reception or baby shower where the atmosphere exudes elegance and sophistication. Refined decor and gentle music facilitate the guests to mingle with glasses of beautifully crafted mocktails in hand. These events often require a touch of class, and thoughtful mocktails can set the tone perfectly. Offering non-alcoholic options ensures everyone feels included, from expectant mothers to health-conscious attendees. Matching the mocktails to the event's theme and colors enhances the overall aesthetic and experience.

One such elegant mocktail is the **Rose and Raspberry Spritzer**. This drink combines rose water's delicate floral notes with the raspberries' tart sweetness. To make it, muddle a handful of raspberries, add some rose water, and fill the glass with sparkling water. Garnish with a few whole raspberries and a rose petal for an exquisite touch. The result is a light, refreshing beverage that pairs beautifully with the refined atmosphere of a wedding or baby shower.

- 1/2 cup fresh raspberries (plus a few extra for garnish)
- 1/2 teaspoon rose water (adjust to taste)
- 1 cup sparkling water
- Ice cubes
- Fresh rose petals for garnish

Here's a splendid recipe for a classic **Cinderella**. Combine the orange, pineapple, and lemon juices in a shaker or glass. Stir or shake well to blend. Pour the grenadine into the mixture, which adds a lovely pink hue and sweetness. Fill the glass with ice and top with soda water or ginger ale for a fizzy finish. For a tropical touch, garnish with an orange slice, pineapple wedge, or maraschino cherry. The festive, colorful appearance of a Cinderella makes it a fun and elegant option for weddings, baby showers, or other celebrations where guests of all ages appreciate mocktails.

- 1/2 cup fresh orange juice
- 1/4 cup fresh pineapple juice
- 1/4 cup fresh lemon juice
- 1 tablespoon grenadine syrup (recipe found in Shirley Temple, Chapter 3.3)
- 1/2 cup soda water or ginger ale
- Ice cubes
- Orange slice, pineapple wedge, or maraschino cherry for garnish

Another sophisticated option is the **Blueberry and Lavender Lemonade**. Combine fresh blueberry puree with freshly squeezed lemon juice and lavender-infused syrup in a pitcher. Fill with cold water and stir well. Serve over ice, garnished with a sprig of lavender and a few whole blueberries. This  mocktail's vibrant color and floral notes make it a standout choice for any elegant gathering. The blueberries' subtle sweetness balances the lemon's tartness, creating a harmonious flavor profile that guests will love. This recipe serves four.

- 1 cup fresh blueberries
- 1 cup freshly squeezed lemon juice
- 1/2 cup lavender-infused syrup (see Chapter 1.5)
- 3 cups cold water
- Ice cubes
- Sprigs of lavender and blueberries for garnish

The **Peach and Jasmine Cooler** is another elegant mocktail. Blend fresh peaches until smooth and mix with a jasmine tea-infused simple syrup. Pour into a glass over ice and top with sparkling water. Garnish with a peach slice and a jasmine flower. The floral notes of jasmine complement the sweetness of the peach, making this drink refreshing and aromatic, ideal for a summer wedding or garden baby shower.

- 1 ripe peach, peeled and chopped
- 2 tablespoons jasmine tea-infused simple syrup (see Chapter 8.1)
- 1 cup sparkling water
- Ice cubes
- Peach slices and jasmine flowers for garnish

Presentation plays a significant role in enhancing the sophistication of these mocktails. Using crystal or vintage glassware can elevate the look of the drinks, making them appear more luxurious. Consider serving the Rose and Raspberry Spritzer in champagne flutes or the Blueberry and Lavender Lemonade in tall, slender glasses. Adding floral and herbal garnishes, such as rose petals, lavender sprigs, or jasmine flowers, enhances the visual appeal and adds an aromatic element to heighten the overall experience. Incorporating pastel colors and delicate decorations can further align the mocktails with the event's theme, creating a cohesive and elegant presentation.

Personalizing the mocktails to fit the theme of the wedding or baby shower can add a unique and memorable touch. Naming the drinks after the couple or baby can make them feel special and create a sense of personalization. For example, you could name the Rose and Raspberry Spritzer "Rose's Delight" for a bride named Rose or the Ginger & Pear Fizz (See Chapter 3.4) "Baby's First Fizz" for a baby shower. Using monogrammed drink stirrers or custom glassware can add an extra layer of elegance. Creating signature mocktails for the event can also make the occasion more exclusive. Work with the couple or parents-to-be to design a drink that reflects their tastes and preferences, making the mocktail menu unique to their celebration.

Imagine a wedding reception where guests receive a beautifully garnished Peach and Jasmine Cooler as they arrive. The delicate aroma of jasmine mingles with the sweet scent of peach, setting a tranquil and celebratory mood. Or picture a baby shower where guests toast the new arrival with glasses of Blueberry and Lavender Lemonade, the vibrant color and floral garnish adding to the joyous atmosphere. These elegant mocktails provide delicious non-alcoholic options and enhance the overall sophistication and personalization of the event.

4.4 FESTIVE MOCKTAILS FOR NEW YEAR'S EVE

New Year's Eve is a celebration filled with joy, hope, and glamor. There's something magical about ringing in the new year with friends and family; the right mocktails can add sparkle and excitement. Special mocktails can create a festive and glamorous atmosphere, offering sophisticated, non-alcoholic options for everyone. Including sparkling and celebratory elements in your drinks can elevate the evening, making each toast feel special.

One of my favorite New Year's Eve mocktails is the **Sparkling Grape and Mint Mocktail**. This drink combines the crisp sweetness of grape juice with the refreshing coolness of mint. To make it, start by muddling fresh mint leaves in a glass. Add grape juice and a splash of lime juice, and fill the glass with ice. Top it off with sparkling water and garnish with a sprig of mint and a few whole grapes. The result is a drink that is both refreshing and celebratory, perfect for toasting to new beginnings.

- 1/2 cup grape juice (white or red)
- 6-8 fresh mint leaves
- 1 tablespoon freshly squeezed lime juice
- 1/2 cup sparkling water
- Ice cubes
- A few whole grapes and a sprig of mint for garnish

Another great option is the **Pomegranate and Lime Fizz**. This mocktail is a beautiful blend of tart pomegranate juice and zesty lime. Combine pomegranate, fresh lime, and a touch of simple syrup in a shaker. Shake well and strain into a glass filled with ice. Top with sparkling water and garnish with pomegranate seeds and a lime wedge. The vibrant red color and the fizzy bubbles make this drink a showstopper at any New Year's Eve party. The pomegranate's tartness and the lime's brightness create a refreshing and invigorating drink that guests will love.

- 1/2 cup pomegranate juice
- 1 tablespoon freshly squeezed lime juice
- 1 tablespoon simple syrup (adjust to taste)
- 1/2 cup sparkling water
- Ice cubes
- Pomegranate seeds and lime wedge for garnish

The **Golden Turmeric and Ginger Spritzer** is a fantastic choice for those who enjoy a bit of spice. This mocktail combines turmeric's anti-inflammatory benefits with ginger's warming spice. Start by making a ginger-turmeric syrup: simmer fresh ginger slices, turmeric powder, and honey in water until syrupy. Let it cool, then mix the syrup with fresh lemon juice and sparkling water. Serve over ice and garnish with a lemon twist and a sprinkle of turmeric powder. The golden color and the complex flavors make this drink visually appealing and delicious. It's a great way to add a healthy twist to your New Year's Eve celebrations.

- 3 tablespoons ginger-turmeric syrup (see below)
- 2 tablespoons freshly squeezed lemon juice
- 1 cup sparkling water
- Ice cubes
- Lemon twist and a sprinkle of turmeric powder for garnish

Ginger-turmeric syrup:

- 2 tablespoons fresh ginger, sliced (or 2 teaspoons dried/ground)
- 1 tablespoon fresh grated turmeric root (or 1 teaspoon dried/ground)
- 1/4 cup honey or maple syrup
- 1/2 cup water

The **Blackberry and Basil Cooler** is another elegant option. In a glass, muddle fresh blackberries with basil leaves. Add a splash of lemon juice and simple syrup. Fill the glass with ice and top with sparkling water. Garnish with a basil sprig and a few whole blackberries. The deep purple color and aromatic basil make this drink beautiful and flavorful, perfect for a glamorous New Year's Eve party.

- 1/4 cup fresh blackberries
- 6-8 fresh basil leaves
- 1 tablespoon freshly squeezed lemon juice
- 1 tablespoon simple syrup (See Chapter 1.5)

- 1 cup sparkling water
- Ice cubes
- Basil sprig and whole blackberries for garnish

Adding sparkle to your New Year's Eve mocktails can make them look festive and dazzling. Using edible glitter or gold flakes can add a touch of magic to your drinks, making them sparkle under the party lights. Adding sparkling water or soda to your mocktails enhances the flavor and adds a festive fizz that makes each sip feel special. Incorporating metallic and jewel-toned garnishes, like gold-rimmed glasses or silver cocktail stirrers, can elevate the presentation and make your mocktails look even more glamorous.

Pairing these festive mocktails with the right appetizers and snacks can enhance the overall experience. The Sparkling Grape and Mint Mocktail pairs wonderfully with cheese platters, the grapes' crispness complementing the cheese's richness. The Golden Turmeric and Ginger Spritzer pairs beautifully with savory canapés, the spice of the ginger enhancing the flavors of the appetizers. The Blackberry and Basil Cooler is a perfect match for chocolate truffles, the blackberries' sweetness complementing the chocolate's decadence. These festive mocktails taste delicious and add a special touch to your New Year's Eve celebrations, making the night even more memorable.

In the next chapter, we will explore mocktails catering to families, offering fun and creative options for everyone. From fizzy fruit punches to kid-friendly smoothies, these drinks bring joy and excitement to family gatherings.

FAMILY-FRIENDLY MOCKTAILS

One sunny afternoon, while preparing for a family gathering, I found myself thinking about how to create drinks that would delight both kids and adults alike. I remembered the joy on my niece's face as she sipped a colorful fruit punch at a previous party, her eyes widening with each fizzy sip. That moment sparked an idea—why not include a whole chapter dedicated to family-friendly mocktails that are fun, delicious, and inclusive? This chapter is about creating mocktails that bring families together, offering something for everyone to enjoy.

5.1 FIZZY FRUIT PUNCHES

Fizzy fruit punches are a hit for kids and adults for several reasons. They combine the sweetness of fruit juices with the effervescence of carbonated water, creating a refreshing and visually appealing drink. The bubbles add a playful element that kids love, while the rich flavors cater to adult palates. These punches are also incredibly easy to make in large batches, making them perfect for family gatherings, birthday parties, and casual get-togethers. The vibrant colors and sparkling bubbles make them a centerpiece at any event, drawing people together to enjoy a delightful beverage.

Creating a **Tropical Pineapple Punch** is a breeze. Start with a base of pineapple juice, which is naturally sweet and tangy. Mix in some coconut water for a hint of tropical flavor. Add a splash of orange juice to balance the sweetness, and top it off with sparkling water for that fizzy effect. Serve it over ice with a garnish of pineapple slices and mint leaves to elevate its visual appeal. This punch is refreshing and packed with vitamins, making it a healthy option for everyone. This recipe makes two servings.

- 1 cup pineapple juice
- 1/2 cup coconut water
- 1/4 cup freshly squeezed orange juice
- 1/2 cup sparkling water
- Ice cubes
- Pineapple slices and mint leaves for garnish

For a **Berry Blast Punch**, combine a mix of berry juices such as strawberry, raspberry, and blueberry. These fruits offer a natural sweetness and a burst of antioxidants. Add a touch of lemon juice to enhance the flavors and give it a zesty kick. Top off the punch with carbonated water for a bubbly finish. Garnish with fresh berries and a sprig of mint. This punch is perfect for summer picnics and outdoor gatherings, offering a refreshing respite from the heat.

- 1/4 cup strawberry juice
- 1/4 cup raspberry juice
- 1/4 cup blueberry juice
- 2 tablespoons freshly squeezed lemon juice
- 1/2 cup sparkling water
- Ice cubes
- Fresh mixed berries (strawberries, raspberries, blueberries) and mint sprigs for garnish

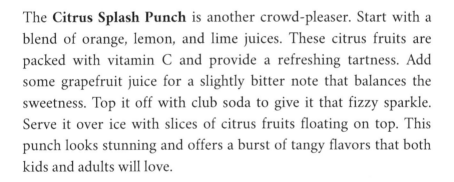

The **Citrus Splash Punch** is another crowd-pleaser. Start with a blend of orange, lemon, and lime juices. These citrus fruits are packed with vitamin C and provide a refreshing tartness. Add some grapefruit juice for a slightly bitter note that balances the sweetness. Top it off with club soda to give it that fizzy sparkle. Serve it over ice with slices of citrus fruits floating on top. This punch looks stunning and offers a burst of tangy flavors that both kids and adults will love.

- 1/2 cup freshly squeezed orange juice
- 2 tablespoons freshly squeezed lemon juice
- 2 tablespoons freshly squeezed lime juice
- 1/4 cup freshly squeezed grapefruit juice
- 1/2 cup club soda
- Ice cubes
- Citrus slices (orange, lemon, lime, grapefruit) for garnish

Add fresh fruit slices and berries to make these punches even more exciting. Not only do they enhance the flavor, but they also make the punch more visually appealing. Using colorful ice cubes can add a fun twist. Freeze pieces of fruit or edible flowers in ice cube trays to create vibrant ice cubes that slowly release flavor as they melt. Garnishing with mint leaves or edible flowers adds an elegant touch that makes the drink feel special.

Keeping these punches low in sugar while maintaining their sweetness and appeal is crucial, especially for health-conscious individuals. Fruit purees are an excellent way to add natural sweetness without relying on added sugars. Simply blend fresh or frozen fruits into a smooth puree and mix it into your punch. This method not only sweetens the drink but also boosts fiber and nutrients. Sweetening with honey or agave syrup is another healthy alternative. Both honey and agave syrup can dissolve in cold liquids and provide a natural sweetness that complements the fruity flavors. Balancing the flavors with a splash of lemon or lime juice can enhance the overall taste, adding a zesty note that makes the punch more refreshing.

Fizzy fruit punches are a delightful addition to any family gathering. They are easy to make, visually appealing, and suit different tastes and dietary needs. Whether hosting a birthday party, a summer barbecue, or simply enjoying a day with family, these punches offer a fun and inclusive way to bring everyone together.

5.2 CREATIVE LEMONADES AND LIMEADES

Lemonades and limeades are cherished for their refreshing and zesty qualities. These classic drinks are versatile and easily customized for any palate or occasion. Whether you're looking for a simple, thirst-quenching beverage on a hot summer day or a more sophisticated concoction to impress your guests, lemonades and limeades are perfect. Their bright, tangy flavors make them a hit with kids and adults, and their adaptability means you can constantly experiment with new ingredients and combinations.

One of my favorite creative twists is **Rainbow Lemonade**. This unique lemonade layers different colors using natural juices and is visually appealing and delicious. Combine freshly squeezed lemon juice, sugar or honey, and cold water. Stir until the sweetener dissolves to create the lemonade base. Set aside the pomegranate, orange, and blueberry juices in separate small bowls or glasses. These will serve as the coloring for different layers. Fill a glass with ice cubes. The ice will help keep the layers separate by slowing the mixing process. Pour the lemonade into the glass, filling it about 1/4 of the way up. Gently pour the orange juice over the back of a spoon so it slowly layers on top of the lemonade. Then, add the blueberry juice in the same way. Finally, gently pour the pomegranate juice over the back of the spoon to create the top layer. Create a colorful fruit skewer using berries, orange slices, or any fruit you like. Garnish each glass with a skewer for extra fun.

- 2 tablespoons freshly squeezed lemon juice
- 2 tablespoons sugar or honey (adjust to taste)
- 1/4 cup cold water
- 1/4 cup pomegranate juice
- 1/4 cup orange juice
- 1/4 cup blueberry juice
- Ice cubes
- Colorful fruit skewers (with strawberries, orange slices, blueberries, etc.) for garnish

Watermelon Limeade is another delightful variation that takes advantage of watermelon's natural sweetness and juiciness. Begin by pureeing fresh watermelon and straining it to remove the pulp. Mix the watermelon juice with freshly squeezed lime juice and a bit of simple syrup if needed. Serve it over ice with a lime wedge and a mint sprig for a refreshing and hydrating treat. This drink is perfect for summer picnics and barbecues, offering a cooling and refreshing flavor.

- 2 cups fresh watermelon, cubed
- 1/4 cup freshly squeezed lime juice
- 1-2 tablespoons simple syrup (optional, adjust to taste)
- Ice cubes
- Lime wedges and mint sprigs for garnish

Here's a kid-friendly recipe for an **Arnold Palmer**. It's perfect for a hot day and offers a nice balance of sweet and tart without caffeine! In a glass, combine the lemonade and decaf iced tea. Stir gently to mix. If you want more sweetness, stir in honey or agave syrup. Fill the glass with ice cubes. Add a lemon slice for garnish if desired.

- 1/2 cup lemonade (store-bought or homemade)
- 1/2 cup iced tea (use decaffeinated tea for kids)
- 1 teaspoon honey or agave syrup (optional for extra sweetness)
- Ice cubes
- Lemon slices for garnish

For a more adventurous palate, try **Blueberry Basil Lemonade**. Combining sweet blueberries and fragrant basil creates a complex and delightful flavor profile. Muddle fresh blueberries with basil leaves in the bottom of a glass, then add lemon juice and simple syrup. Top it off with cold water or sparkling water and serve over ice. Dilute to taste. Garnish with a few whole blueberries and a basil leaf for a visually stunning and delicious drink. This lemonade is great for brunches or garden parties, adding a touch of sophistication to any gathering.

- 1/4 cup fresh blueberries (plus extra for garnish)
- 5-6 fresh basil leaves (plus extra for garnish)
- 1/4 cup freshly squeezed lemon juice
- 1/4 cup simple syrup (adjust to taste)
- 1 cup cold water or sparkling water
- Ice cubes
- Basil leaf and whole blueberries for garnish

Customizing these lemonades and limeades to suit different tastes is part of the fun. Adjusting the sweetness levels is a simple yet effective way to tailor the drink to your preference. If you prefer a less sweet beverage, reduce the sweetener or use a natural alternative like honey or agave syrup. For those who enjoy a sweeter drink, add a bit more simple syrup or even a splash of fruit juice. Adding herbs and spices can also elevate the flavor. Fresh herbs like mint, basil, and rosemary add aromatic complexity, while spices like ginger and cinnamon can introduce warmth and depth. Mixing with other fruit juices like orange, grapefruit, or cranberry can create new flavor combinations. For example, adding a splash of grapefruit juice to your lemonade can enhance its tartness and add bitterness for a more grown-up taste.

Presentation is significant in making these drinks memorable, especially for family gatherings. Serving lemonade and limeade in mason jars adds a rustic charm that is both inviting and practical.

Using decorative straws, such as colorful paper or reusable metal straws, can make the drinks more fun and visually appealing, particularly for kids. Garnishing with citrus slices, fresh herbs, or even edible flowers can transform a simple drink into a beautiful centerpiece. Imagine a row of mason jars on a picnic table filled with vibrant lemonades and garnished with a slice of lemon and a sprig of mint. The visual appeal is undeniable, making the drinks even more enticing.

Creative lemonades and limeades are refreshing, delicious, and endlessly customizable. They offer a perfect canvas for experimenting with flavors, making them ideal for any occasion. Whether hosting a family barbecue, celebrating a birthday, or simply enjoying a sunny afternoon, these drinks will bring joy to everyone.

5.3 KID-FRIENDLY SMOOTHIES AND SHAKES

Kid-friendly smoothies and shakes are excellent ways to incorporate nutrition into a child's diet. These drinks are nutrient-dense, fun, and delicious, making them a favorite among kids and parents. Imagine starting your child's day with a smoothie packed with vitamins and minerals disguised as a tasty treat. It's an easy and effective way to ensure they get essential nutrients without a fuss. Smoothies and shakes also allow for endless creativity, letting you sneak in healthy ingredients that kids might otherwise avoid. They're quick to prepare, making them perfect for busy mornings or as an afternoon snack.

One of my most beloved recipes is the **Banana & Peanut Butter Smoothie**. This drink combines the natural sweetness of bananas with peanut butter's rich, creamy texture. To make it, blend a ripe banana, a tablespoon of peanut butter, a cup of milk (or a dairy alternative), and a bit of honey. The result is a satisfying and nutritious smoothie packed with protein and potassium.

- 1 ripe banana
- 1 tablespoon peanut butter (smooth or crunchy)
- 1 cup milk (or a dairy alternative like almond, oat, or soy milk)
- 1-2 teaspoons honey (adjust to taste)
- 1/4 teaspoon vanilla extract (optional for extra flavor)
- Ice cubes (optional for a colder smoothie)

Another favorite is the **Strawberry & Yogurt Shake**. Blend fresh or frozen strawberries with a cup of yogurt, a splash of milk, and a drizzle of honey. This shake is delicious and rich in probiotics, which support gut health.

- 1/2 cup fresh or frozen strawberries
- 1 cup plain or Greek yogurt
- 1/2 cup milk (or a dairy alternative like almond or oat milk)
- 1-2 teaspoons honey (adjust to taste)
- 1/4 teaspoon vanilla extract (optional for extra flavor)
- Ice cubes (optional for a thicker, colder shake)

For a more decadent option, try the **Chocolate Avocado Smoothie**. Blend half an avocado with a tablespoon of cocoa powder, a banana, a cup of milk, and a touch of honey. The avocado adds a creamy texture and healthy fats, while the cocoa provides a chocolatey richness that kids love.

- 1/2 ripe avocado
- 1 ripe banana
- 1 tablespoon cocoa powder (unsweetened)
- 1 cup milk (or a dairy alternative like almond, oat, or soy milk)
- 1-2 teaspoons honey (adjust to taste)
- 1/4 teaspoon vanilla extract (optional for extra flavor)
- Ice cubes (optional for a colder smoothie)

Enhancing the flavor and texture of these smoothies and shakes is vital to making them more appealing. Adding a handful of spinach to a smoothie is an easy way to incorporate hidden greens. The mild flavor of spinach blends seamlessly with fruits like bananas and berries, adding nutrients without altering the taste. Using frozen fruits can also make your smoothies thicker and more refreshing. Imagine the creamy texture of a strawberry shake made with frozen strawberries, perfect for a hot day. Incorporating fun flavors like vanilla or cocoa can elevate the drink even further. A splash of vanilla extract can add depth to a banana smoothie, while a spoonful of cocoa powder can turn an ordinary shake into a chocolate delight.

Consider allergy-friendly options to ensure inclusivity. Many kids have allergies to common ingredients like dairy and nuts, but plenty of alternatives exist. Using almond or oat milk instead of regular milk can cater to those with lactose intolerance or dairy allergies. Both almond and oat milk provide a creamy texture and a slightly nutty flavor that complements most smoothies. Replacing peanut butter with sunflower seed butter is another excellent option. Sunflower seed butter has a similar texture and taste but is safe for those with nut allergies. For children under one year old, avoiding honey is a good idea, as it can pose a risk of botulism. Instead, you can use agave syrup or maple syrup for sweetness.

Imagine preparing a snack for a group of kids with varying dietary needs. You whip up Strawberry and Yogurt Shakes using almond milk and sunflower seed butter. The kids are delighted by the sweet, creamy treat, and you can rest easy knowing that everyone can enjoy it safely.

Kid-friendly smoothies and shakes are nutritious, versatile, and easy to prepare. They offer a fun and delicious way to ensure your kids get the nutrients they need while catering to different dietary preferences and allergies. Whether starting the day with a Banana and Peanut Butter Smoothie or treating your kids to a Chocolate Avocado Shake, these drinks will be a hit.

5.4 POPSICLES: REFRESHING TREATS

Turning mocktails into frozen treats instantly makes them more fun and refreshing, especially on hot days. Mocktail popsicles offer a delightful twist to traditional beverages, transforming them into icy delights that are easy to enjoy. The appeal lies in their versatility and the joy of eating something cold and flavorful. Imagine a sweltering summer afternoon. As the sun blazes down, everyone craves something icy and refreshing. A batch of homemade mocktail popsicles can be the perfect solution, offering flavor and coolness with each bite.

Creating **Tropical Mango Coconut Popsicles** is a straightforward yet rewarding endeavor. Start by blending ripe mango chunks with coconut milk until smooth. The mango's natural sweetness pairs beautifully with the coconut milk's creamy texture, creating a tropical flavor that is both rich and refreshing. Pour the mixture into popsicle molds, insert sticks, and freeze until solid. These popsicles are a tropical escape in every bite, transporting you to a sunny beach with swaying palm trees.

- 2 ripe mangoes, peeled and chopped (about 2 cups)
- 1 cup coconut milk (full-fat for creamier popsicles)
- 1-2 tablespoons honey or maple syrup (adjust to taste)

Berry Lemonade Popsicles are another crowd-pleaser. Combine freshly squeezed lemon juice and water with a berry puree made from strawberries, blueberries, or raspberries. Add a touch of honey or agave syrup to sweeten the mixture naturally. Pour the berry lemonade into molds and freeze.  The result is a vibrant, tangy popsicle that bursts with berry flavor. These are perfect for kids' birthday parties or a healthy treat on a hot day.

- 1/2 cup freshly squeezed lemon juice
- 1 cup mixed berries (strawberries, blueberries, raspberries)
- 1/4 cup honey or agave syrup (adjust to taste)
- 1 cup water

Minty Watermelon Popsicles are a refreshing and hydrating option. Start by pureeing fresh watermelon chunks and mixing in finely chopped mint leaves. The mint adds a cooling effect that enhances the watermelon's natural sweetness. Pour the mixture into molds, and for an added twist, try layering it with a splash of lime juice for a bit of tartness. Freeze until solid, and you'll have a delightful, icy treat that kids and adults love.

- 2 cups fresh watermelon chunks
- 1-2 tablespoons finely chopped fresh mint leaves
- 1/4 cup freshly squeezed lime juice
- 1-2 tablespoons honey or agave syrup (adjust to taste)

When making popsicles, use ripe fruits to ensure natural sweetness, eliminating the need for added sugars. If the fruit is not as sweet as you'd like, a splash of juice or coconut water can enhance the flavor while keeping the popsicles hydrating and refreshing. Layering different flavors makes the popsicles more visually appealing and adds complexity to each bite. For instance, layering mango puree with coconut milk creates a beautiful contrast and a richer taste experience.

Proper storage and serving tips can significantly improve the enjoyment of your popsicles. Freezing techniques are crucial; ensure that your freezer is set to the right temperature to avoid ice crystals forming in the popsicles, which can affect their texture. Adding a little cornstarch to the mix can also help to prevent ice crystals, producing a creamier finished product.

Using silicone molds can make the release process more effortless and prevent the popsicles from sticking. Simply run the molds under warm water for a few seconds to loosen the popsicles. Serving them with fun popsicle sticks or colorful paper straws can create excitement, especially for kids. You can also wrap the popsicles individually in plastic wrap and store them in a freezer bag to keep them fresh and ready to enjoy at any time.

Imagine the delight on your kids' faces as they enjoy a minty watermelon popsicle after a long day of playing outside. The icy treat cools them down instantly, and the burst of fresh flavors keeps them returning for more. These moments are made special with simple yet thoughtfully crafted popsicles that cater to everyone's tastes and preferences.

Popsicles are a fun and creative way to enjoy, offering a refreshing twist perfect for hot days. They are easy to make with simple ingredients and suit any flavor preference. Whether preparing a batch for a family gathering or looking for a healthy treat on a sunny afternoon, these are always a hit.

HEALTH-CONSCIOUS MOCKTAILS

One sunny afternoon, I returned from the local farmers' market with fresh fruit baskets. The vibrant colors and fragrant aromas inspired me to create something refreshing and wholesome. That day, I experimented with infusing water with a variety of fruits. The resulting drinks brought a sense of wellness and vitality. This experiment began my journey into the world of low-sugar fruit infusions, a delightful way to enjoy mocktails without the added sugars.

6.1 FRUIT INFUSIONS

Fruit infusions naturally add sweetness and flavor to your drinks without relying on added sugars. They are perfect for health-conscious individuals looking to reduce sugar intake. Infusing water with berries is a beautiful place to start. Berries like strawberries, blueberries, and raspberries are packed with antioxidants, providing a subtle sweetness that can transform plain water into a refreshing beverage. Imagine the burst of flavor from a handful of ripe berries, their juices melding with the water to create a hydrating and delicious drink.

Citrus slices are another fantastic option for infusions. The zestiness of lemon, lime, or orange slices adds a bright, refreshing kick to your drink. The natural acidity of citrus fruits enhances the flavor and offers health benefits like improved digestion and a boost of vitamin C.

Making fruit infusions is straightforward and requires minimal effort. Start by slicing your chosen fruits and placing them in a pitcher or jar. The size and thickness of the slices will affect the infusion time, with thinner slices releasing flavor more quickly. Fill the container with cold water and let it sit in the refrigerator for a few hours, depending on how strong you want the flavor. Aim for an infusion time of at least two hours for optimal results. If you prefer a more intense flavor, let it sit longer, but be mindful that some fruits may become mushy if left for too long.

Proper storage will maintain the freshness of your infused water. Keep the pitcher covered in the refrigerator and consume it within two to three days for the best taste. If you're making a large batch, consider removing the fruit after the initial infusion period to prevent it from breaking down and altering the flavor.

Here are a few fruit infusion recipes to get you started. First, try a **Cucumber and Mint Water**. Thinly slice half a cucumber and add it to a pitcher of water, along with a handful of fresh mint leaves. Let it infuse for at least two hours. This combination is incredibly refreshing and perfect for hot summer days.

Another option is a **Strawberry and Basil Infusion**. Add a cup of strawberries to a pitcher with a handful of basil leaves. The sweetness of the strawberries pairs beautifully with the aromatic notes of basil, creating a sophisticated and delicious drink.

Lastly, consider **Lemon and Ginger Water**. Thinly slice a lemon and a small piece of fresh ginger, adding both to a water pitcher. This infusion offers a zesty kick with a hint of warmth from the ginger, making it an excellent choice for boosting your immunity and aiding digestion.

Fruit infusions are incredibly versatile. Adding them to sparkling water creates a fizzy, flavorful drink perfect for special occasions or simply to make your daily hydration more exciting. You can also freeze fruit-infused water into ice cubes. These cubes keep your drink cold and add flavor as they melt, ensuring your last sip is as delicious as the first. Creating layered drinks with infusions is another fun option. For example, start with a base of lemon and ginger water, then add a splash of cucumber mint infusion for a multi-layered experience that evolves with each sip.

Fruit infusions are a delightful way to enjoy healthy, flavorful drinks without added sugars. They offer endless possibilities for creativity to suit any occasion or preference.

6.2 HERBAL AND BOTANICAL BLENDS

Herbs and botanicals can transform a simple mocktail into an aromatic and flavorful experience. Herbs like mint, basil, and rosemary provide freshness, while botanicals such as lavender and chamomile add unique flavors and benefits. Using fresh herbs not only elevates the taste but also introduces health-boosting properties. For instance, mint is known for its digestive benefits, and basil offers anti-inflammatory qualities. Common botanicals like chamomile can promote relaxation, making your mocktails delicious and functional.

Adaptogens like ashwagandha and holy basil help the body manage stress levels and promote well-being. These herbs have been used in traditional medicine for centuries to support mental clarity and reduce anxiety. Ashwagandha, for instance, is known for its ability to lower cortisol levels, which can help reduce stress and improve mood. Holy basil, known as tulsi, is revered in Ayurvedic medicine for its calming and therapeutic properties. Experiment with adding these lesser-known herbs to your recipes.

Try the **Lavender Lemon Basil Cooler** for a calming yet zesty drink with an herbal twist. Muddle basil leaves in the bottom of a glass to release their flavor. Add lavender syrup and lemon juice, then top with ice. Pour sparkling water over and gently stir. Garnish with a lemon twist and a basil sprig for aromatics. Pro Tip: Infuse the lavender syrup with a hint of rosemary for added depth.

- 2 tablespoons lavender syrup (See Chapter 1.5)
- 6-8 fresh basil leaves, lightly muddled
- 2 tablespoons fresh lemon juice
- 1 cup sparkling water

If you'd prefer a cooling, refreshing blend with calming chamomile undertones, try a **Cucumber Mint Chamomile Spritz**. Muddle mint leaves in a shaker, then add chamomile tea, cucumber juice, and lime juice. Shake with ice and strain into a glass filled with ice.

Top with soda water and garnish with a cucumber slice and a mint sprig. Pro Tip: Add a dash of elderflower syrup for a subtle floral sweetness.

- 1/2 cup chamomile tea (brewed and chilled)
- 1/4 cup cucumber juice (freshly pressed)
- 2 tablespoons fresh lime juice
- 6-8 fresh mint leaves
- 1/2 cup soda water
- Cucumber slice and mint sprig for garnish

The **Rosemary Ginger Citrus Tonic** is a bright, refreshing mocktail combining ginger's warmth with rosemary's piney notes. Gently bruise the rosemary sprig to release its oils and place it in a glass. Add orange juice, grapefruit juice, and ginger syrup, then stir. Fill the glass with ice and top with tonic water. Garnish with an orange peel twist and a small rosemary sprig for a fragrant finish. Pro Tip: Lightly torch the rosemary before garnishing for a smoky aroma that complements the ginger.

- 1/4 cup fresh orange juice
- 1/4 cup grapefruit juice
- 2 tablespoons ginger syrup (See Chapter 1.5)
- 1/2 cup tonic water
- 1 sprig of fresh rosemary
- Orange peel twist for garnish

Herbs and botanicals enhance flavor and offer a range of health benefits. Turmeric, for example, is a potent anti-inflammatory and can be added to mocktails for a health boost. Ginger aids digestion and adds a spicy kick to your drinks. Chamomile has relaxing properties, making it an excellent choice for evening mocktails. By incorporating these ingredients, you can create tasty drinks that support your overall well-being. Herbal and botanical blends offer endless possibilities for creativity. You can experiment with different combinations to find what suits your taste.

6.3 SUPERFOOD SMOOTHIES: NUTRIENT-RICH OPTIONS

Superfoods are powerhouse ingredients packed with nutrients and known for their numerous health benefits. Rich in vitamins, minerals, and antioxidants, these foods can make a significant impact on your daily diet. Common superfoods, such as blueberries, chia seeds, spirulina, and acai berries, offer many advantages. Blueberries, for instance, are loaded with antioxidants and vitamin C, which combat free radicals and promote healthy skin. Chia seeds, high in omega-3 fatty acids and fiber, support heart health and digestion. Spirulina, a type of blue-green algae, stands out as an excellent source of protein. Acai berries, often enjoyed in smoothie bowls, provide a boost of antioxidants and healthy fats. Incorporating superfoods into your smoothies can elevate your nutrient intake and support your overall health.

Creating a nutrient-rich smoothie that tastes great involves balancing flavors and textures. Start with a liquid base like almond milk or coconut water. These options add a creamy texture without the heaviness of dairy. For sweetness, consider using natural sweeteners such as dates or honey to keep your smoothie free from refined sugars while adding depth of flavor. Balance the flavors by combining sweet fruits with more neutral or bitter greens. For example, blending spinach with pineapple provides a sweet yet earthy taste. Adding a handful of nuts or seeds can give your smoothie a satisfying crunch and an extra dose of healthy fats and protein.

One of my favorite superfood smoothie recipes is the **Blueberry and Chia Seed Smoothie**. Combine a cup of blueberries, a tablespoon of chia seeds, a banana, and almond milk in a blender. Blend until smooth. This smoothie is delicious and rich in antioxidants and fiber, making it a perfect start to your day.

- 1/2 cup fresh or frozen blueberries
- 1 tablespoon chia seeds
- 1 ripe banana
- 1 cup almond milk (or any milk of your choice)
- Ice cubes (optional for a colder smoothie)

Another great option is the **Green Smoothie with Spirulina**. Mix a handful of spinach, a teaspoon of spirulina powder, half an avocado, a kiwi, and a cup of coconut water. The result is a vibrant green drink packed with nutrients.

- 1 cup fresh spinach
- 1 teaspoon spirulina powder
- 1/2 ripe avocado
- 1 kiwi, peeled and chopped
- 1 cup coconut water
- Ice cubes (optional for a chilled smoothie)

For a more exotic flavor, try the **Acai and Banana Blend**. Blend a packet of frozen acai puree with a banana, a handful of mixed berries, and a cup of orange juice. This smoothie is a delicious way to enjoy the benefits of acai berries, known for their high antioxidant content.

- 1 packet of frozen acai puree
- 1 ripe banana
- 1/2 cup mixed berries (strawberries, blueberries, raspberries)
- 1 cup orange juice
- Ice cubes (optional for a thicker blend)

Each of these smoothies offers specific health benefits. The Blueberry and Chia Seed Smoothie supports heart health and digestion. Blueberries provide antioxidants, while chia seeds offer omega-3 fatty acids and fiber. The Green Smoothie with Spirulina is a nutrient-dense option that supports detoxification and boosts energy levels. Spirulina is rich in protein and essential amino acids, making it an excellent addition to your diet. The Acai and Banana Blend is perfect for boosting your immune system and providing a quick energy boost. Acai berries contain antioxidants and healthy fats, making this smoothie delicious and nutritious.

6.4 DETOXIFYING MOCKTAILS

Detoxifying mocktails are a refreshing way to cleanse your body and support overall health. Detoxification helps remove toxins from processed foods, environmental pollutants, and everyday stress. These toxins can burden your liver and kidneys, the organs responsible for filtering and eliminating waste. By aiding these natural detox processes, detoxifying mocktails can help improve digestion, boost energy levels, and enhance skin health. Imagine starting your day with a drink that tastes delicious and supports your liver and kidneys, helping them function more efficiently.

Key ingredients can significantly enhance the detoxifying properties of your mocktails. Lemons are a fantastic choice, packed with vitamin C and antioxidants. They help detoxify the body by stimulating liver function and promoting bile production, which aids digestion. Cucumber is another excellent detox ingredient. Its high water content ensures hydration, while its soothing properties help flush out toxins and reduce inflammation. Activated charcoal, though less common, is highly effective at binding to toxins and removing them from the body. This ingredient can be beneficial for a more intensive detox.

Here are some simple detoxifying mocktail recipes to get you started. First, try **Lemon Cucumber Detox Water.** Combine thinly sliced lemons and cucumbers in a large pitcher with cold water. Let it sit in the fridge for a few hours to infuse, then enjoy. This drink is incredibly hydrating and refreshing, perfect for any time of day. Another option is **Activated Charcoal Lemonade**. Mix activated charcoal powder with fresh lemon juice, water, and honey. This dramatic, black-hued drink is visually striking and powerful in removing toxins. For a more nutrient-packed option, consider a **Green Detox Smoothie**. Blend a handful of spinach, a small cucumber, a green apple, and a cup of coconut water. This smoothie is rich in vitamins and minerals, providing a gentle yet effective detox.

To maximize the benefits of detoxifying mocktails, consider drinking them first thing in the morning. This practice kickstarts your metabolism and helps flush out toxins accumulated overnight. Staying hydrated throughout the day is equally important. Sipping on detoxifying mocktails can make hydration more enjoyable, encouraging you to drink more fluids. These drinks can be a delightful addition to your daily routine, offering flavor and health benefits.

6.5 IMMUNE-BOOSTING MOCKTAILS

Immune-boosting mocktails can play a vital role in fortifying your body's defenses. They contain ingredients that help fight off infections and reduce the duration of illnesses, giving your immune system the support it needs to keep you healthy. Imagine sipping on a refreshing drink that tastes great and strengthens your body's natural defenses.

Certain ingredients are essential for crafting these potent beverages. Ginger is a standout, celebrated for its anti-inflammatory and antioxidant properties. It adds a spicy kick and helps reduce inflammation and combat oxidative stress. Pure ginger shots have become a popular drink. Turmeric is another powerhouse known for boosting immune response. Its active compound, curcumin, has been shown to enhance the body's ability to fight pathogens. Citrus fruits like lemons, oranges, and grapefruits are high in vitamin C, a crucial nutrient for immune health. They provide a zesty flavor while delivering potent antioxidants that support immune function and skin health.

One of my go-to recipes is the **Ginger Turmeric Tonic**. This drink combines fresh ginger and turmeric roots with lemon juice and honey. Simmer them together for 10 minutes, strain, and cool before stirring in the lemon juice and honey. The ginger provides a warming sensation, while the turmeric adds an earthy depth. Together, they create a tonic that is both invigorating and health-boosting.

- 2 tablespoons fresh ginger, sliced (or 2 teaspoons dried/ground)
- 1 tablespoon fresh grated turmeric root (or 1 teaspoon dried/ground)
- 2 tablespoons freshly squeezed lemon juice
- 1 tablespoon honey (adjust to taste)
- 2 cups water

Another favorite is the **Citrus Immunity Booster.** This mocktail blends orange juice, grapefruit juice, and a touch of lime over ice, creating a vibrant and tangy drink loaded with vitamin C.

- 1/2 cup freshly squeezed orange juice
- 1/2 cup freshly squeezed grapefruit juice
- 1 tablespoon freshly squeezed lime juice
- 1 teaspoon honey or agave syrup
- Ice cubes
- Citrus slices (orange, grapefruit, lime) for garnish

Use fresh, organic ingredients to maximize the immune-boosting effects of these mocktails. Fresh produce retains more nutrients and is free from harmful pesticides. Adding a pinch of black pepper to turmeric-based drinks can significantly enhance the absorption of curcumin, making the turmeric more effective. Black pepper contains piperine, a compound that increases the bioavailability of curcumin, ensuring you get the most benefit from your drink. These minor adjustments can significantly affect how well your body absorbs and utilizes the nutrients. Whether you're looking to fend off a cold, reduce inflammation, or simply give your immune system extra support, these mocktails offer a convenient and enjoyable solution.

6.6 DIGESTIVE HEALTH: MOCKTAILS FOR GUT WELLNESS

Digestive health is a cornerstone of overall well-being. A healthy gut supports nutrient absorption, ensuring your body gets the vitamins and minerals from food. It also improves bowel regularity, which helps eliminate waste and toxins. When your digestive system functions optimally, you feel more energetic and less bloated, and your immune system operates more efficiently.

Certain ingredients are known for their gut-friendly properties. Aloe vera, for instance, is soothing and hydrating. It can help reduce inflammation in the digestive tract, making it an excellent addition to your digestive health mocktails. Ginger shines here as well, well-known for aiding digestion and reducing nausea. Its spicy warmth can be incredibly comforting and effective in settling an upset stomach. Probiotic-rich ingredients like kombucha and kefir introduce beneficial bacteria to your gut, promoting a balanced microbiome and improving digestion. These ingredients support your digestive health and add unique flavors and textures to your drinks.

Consider a simple yet effective recipe like **Aloe Vera Lemonade**. Start by extracting the gel from an aloe vera leaf and blending it with fresh lemon juice and water. Add a touch of honey for sweetness. This drink is refreshing and incredibly soothing for your digestive system.

- 2 tablespoons fresh aloe vera gel (extracted from an aloe vera leaf)
- 1/4 cup freshly squeezed lemon juice

- 1 cup water
- 2 tablespoons honey (adjust to taste)
- Ice cubes
- Lemon slices for garnish

Another great option is the **Ginger Mint Digestive Aid**. Combine freshly grated ginger, mint leaves, and a splash of lime juice in a glass of water. Muddle the ingredients gently to release their flavors, then top with sparkling water. This mocktail is perfect for sipping before meals to stimulate digestion.

- 1-inch piece of fresh ginger, grated
- 6-8 fresh mint leaves
- 1 tablespoon freshly squeezed lime juice
- 1 cup water (still or sparkling)
- Ice cubes
- Mint sprig and lime wedge for garnish

For a probiotic boost, try the **Kombucha Berry Fizz**. Mix your favorite berry-flavored kombucha with a handful of sliced fresh berries and a sprig of mint. The kombucha's effervescence, combined with the fresh berries, makes for a delightful and gut-friendly drink.

- 1 cup berry-flavored kombucha
- 1/4 cup fresh mixed berries (strawberries, blueberries, raspberries)
- 1 sprig of fresh mint (plus extra for garnish)
- Ice cubes
- Extra berries for garnish

To enhance the digestive benefits of these mocktails, consider drinking them before meals. This practice can help stimulate digestive enzymes and prepare your stomach for food. Avoiding high-sugar ingredients is also crucial, as excessive sugar can disrupt gut flora and lead to digestive issues. Stick to natural sweeteners like honey or agave syrup in moderation. These minor adjustments can significantly affect how well your digestive system functions, allowing you to enjoy your mocktails while supporting your gut health.

6.7 ENERGY-BOOSTING MOCKTAILS

Natural energy sources are helpful on those long days when you need to stay alert and active without relying on caffeine-heavy or sugar-laden drinks. Unlike these quick fixes, energy-boosting mocktails offer sustained energy without the inevitable crashes, supporting your overall vitality. They nourish your body with natural ingredients that provide a steady release of energy, keeping you focused and refreshed throughout the day.

Key ingredients can make all the difference in your energy levels. Matcha, a finely ground green tea powder, is known for its slow-release caffeine and high antioxidant content, meaning you get a gentle, sustained energy boost without the jitters. Ginseng, another powerful ingredient, enhances both energy and mental performance. It's often used in traditional medicine to fight fatigue and improve concentration. Maca, a root vegetable from the Andes, is celebrated for its ability to boost stamina and endurance. It adds a nutty flavor to your mocktails while providing a natural energy lift.

One refreshing recipe to try is **Matcha Lemonade**. Start by whisking a teaspoon of matcha powder with hot water to dissolve it. Then, mix it with fresh lemon juice, cold water, and a touch of honey. Serve over ice for a revitalizing drink that keeps you energized and alert.

- 1 teaspoon matcha powder
- 2 tablespoons hot water (not boiling)
- 2 tablespoons fresh lemon juice
- 1 tablespoon honey (adjust to taste)
- 1 cup cold water
- Ice cubes
- Lemon slices for garnish

Another excellent option is the **Ginseng Citrus Spritz**. Combine ginseng tea with fresh orange and lemon juice, then add sparkling water for a refreshing drink.

- 1 cup brewed ginseng tea (chilled)
- 1/4 cup fresh orange juice
- 2 tablespoons fresh lemon juice
- 1 tablespoon honey or agave syrup (optional, to taste)
- 1/2 cup sparkling water
- Ice cubes
- Orange or lemon slices for garnish

The **Maca Berry Smoothie** is a fantastic choice for something a bit richer. Blend a teaspoon of maca powder with a cup of mixed berries, a banana, and almond milk. This smoothie tastes delicious and provides a steady energy boost to power you through your day.

- 1 teaspoon maca powder
- 1/2 cup mixed berries (fresh or frozen; blueberries, strawberries, raspberries, etc.)
- 1 ripe banana

- 1 cup almond milk (or any preferred milk)
- 1 teaspoon honey or maple syrup (optional for sweetness)
- Ice cubes (optional for a thicker texture)

Maintaining energy levels involves more than just the drinks you consume. Combining energy-boosting ingredients with hydrating bases like coconut water is essential to hydrate your body. Consuming balanced meals and snacks throughout the day can also help sustain your energy. Foods rich in protein, healthy fats, and complex carbohydrates provide a slow and steady release of energy, preventing the peaks and troughs that come with sugar-heavy snacks. Integrating these practices into your routine allows you to enjoy consistent energy levels and improved overall well-being.

In the next chapter, we'll explore mocktails catering to expectant mothers, offering safe and delicious options that ensure everyone can join the celebration. From refreshing citrus blends to nourishing smoothies, these recipes will provide a variety of enjoyable and beneficial choices.

PREGNANCY-SAFE MOCKTAILS

I once prepared drinks for a group of expectant mothers following a prenatal yoga class. At the event, I noticed the sheer joy on their faces as they sipped the refreshing, non-alcoholic beverages and discussed their experiences. It was a heartwarming sight, knowing that these mocktails provided enjoyment and essential nutrients. That experience inspired me to create a collection of pregnancy-safe mocktails that are delicious and beneficial for both mother and baby.

7.1 NOURISHING SMOOTHIES FOR MOMS-TO-BE

Smoothies offer a marvelous way to pack essential nutrients into one delicious drink, making them an ideal choice for expectant mothers. They are incredibly versatile, allowing you to blend fruits, vegetables, nuts, and seeds into a nutrient-dense beverage. Increased fiber content is one of the health advantages of smoothies, helping to keep your digestive system running smoothly. During pregnancy, constipation can be a common issue, and fiber-rich smoothies can help alleviate this discomfort. Moreover, smoothies can be a great source of protein, which is crucial for the growth and development of your baby. Protein helps build tissues and organs, including the brain. Healthy fats like those in avocados and nuts are also essential for brain development and overall health.

One of my favorite smoothie recipes is the **Avocado and Spinach Smoothie**. Avocado is rich in healthy fats and provides a creamy texture, making this smoothie incredibly satisfying. Start by blending half an avocado with a handful of fresh spinach, almond milk, and a splash of lime juice. Add a teaspoon of honey for sweetness and a few ice cubes. This smoothie tastes great and delivers a powerhouse of nutrients, including vitamins A, C, and E, as well as folate and potassium. The spinach adds fiber and iron, making this drink a perfect choice for a nutritious boost.

- 1/2 ripe avocado
- 1 handful fresh spinach
- 1 cup almond milk (or your preferred milk)
- 1 tablespoon freshly squeezed lime juice
- 1 teaspoon honey
- Ice cubes (optional for a chilled smoothie)

Another delicious option is the **Banana and Almond Butter Blend**. Bananas are rich in potassium, which helps maintain proper fluid balance and supports muscle function. Combine one ripe banana in a blender with a tablespoon of almond butter, a cup of oat milk, and a teaspoon of chia seeds. Add a drizzle of honey and blend until smooth. This smoothie is creamy and satisfying, offering a good mix of protein, healthy fats, and fiber. The chia seeds add an extra dose of omega-3 fatty acids essential for brain development.

- 1 ripe banana
- 1 tablespoon almond butter
- 1 cup oat milk (or your preferred milk)
- 1 teaspoon chia seeds
- 1 teaspoon honey
- Ice cubes (optional for a chilled drink)

Try the **Berry and Greek Yogurt Smoothie** for a fruity and tangy option. Berries contain antioxidants that help protect your cells from damage. Combine a cup of mixed berries (strawberries, blueberries, and raspberries) with half a cup of Greek yogurt, a tablespoon of flaxseeds, and a splash of orange  juice. Blend until smooth, and enjoy this vibrant, nutrient-packed drink. The Greek yogurt provides protein and calcium, while the flaxseeds add fiber and omega-3 fatty acids. This smoothie is not only delicious but also incredibly nourishing.

- 1 cup mixed berries (strawberries, blueberries, raspberries)
- 1/2 cup Greek yogurt
- 1 tablespoon flaxseeds
- 1/2 cup orange juice (or more, to adjust consistency)
- Ice cubes (optional for a chilled smoothie)

Add superfoods like chia seeds or flaxseeds to make your smoothies even more nutritious. These seeds are rich in omega-3 fatty acids, fiber, and protein, making them a valuable addition to any smoothie. Incorporating leafy greens like spinach, kale, or Swiss chard can boost your drink's vitamin and mineral content. These greens are high in iron, calcium, and folate, essential for a healthy pregnancy. Using fortified plant-based milk, such as almond or oat, can add extra vitamins and minerals, including calcium and vitamin D.

When preparing smoothies during pregnancy, remember to choose safe ingredients. Avoid using raw eggs or unpasteurized dairy products, as they can carry harmful bacteria. Opt for pasteurized dairy or plant-based alternatives to ensure safety. Always use well-washed fruits and vegetables to reduce the risk of contamination. If you're using protein powders, ensure they are formulated for pregnancy. Some protein powders may contain unsafe ingredients for expectant mothers, so reading labels and choosing wisely is essential.

Incorporating smoothies into your daily routine can be a simple and effective way to ensure you're getting a balanced intake of nutrients. They are delightful anytime, whether as a breakfast option, a midday snack, or a post-dinner treat. The flexibility of smoothies allows you to experiment with different flavors and ingredients, keeping your diet varied and enjoyable. Whether you prefer the creamy texture of an Avocado and Spinach Smoothie, the nutty richness of a Banana and Almond Butter Blend, or the fruity tang of a Berry and Greek Yogurt Smoothie, there's a smoothie to suit every taste and nutritional need.

7.2 HERBAL TEAS AND INFUSIONS FOR PREGNANCY

Herbal teas can be an excellent addition to your pregnancy routine, offering a range of benefits from relaxation to digestive support. Chamomile, for instance, is renowned for its calming effects. It helps reduce anxiety and promotes better sleep, making it a perfect choice for those restless nights. Chamomile is also gentle on the stomach, providing a soothing experience that can help ease mild digestive discomfort. Peppermint, on the other hand, is a fantastic digestive aid. It helps relax the digestive tract muscles, reducing bloating and gas. Many expectant mothers find peppermint tea particularly helpful in alleviating morning sickness. Ginger tea is another ally in the fight against nausea. The spicy warmth of ginger can soothe an upset stomach and reduce the frequency and severity of nausea, a common issue during pregnancy.

Creating herbal infusions at home can be both enjoyable and beneficial. A **Chamomile and Lavender Blend** is a delightful way to unwind at the end of the day. Start by boiling dried chamomile flowers and lavender buds for about five minutes. Strain the mixture and sweeten it with a touch of honey if desired. This blend calms the mind and offers a floral aroma that enhances the overall experience.

- 2 teaspoons dried chamomile flowers
- 2 teaspoons dried lavender buds
- 1 cup boiling water
- 1 teaspoon honey (adjust to taste)

For a refreshing option, try a **Mint and Lemon Balm Infusion**. Combine a handful of fresh mint leaves with a few lemon balm leaves and steep in hot water for about five to seven minutes. The result is a light, invigorating tea that helps soothe the digestive system while providing a calming effect.

- 8-10 fresh mint leaves
- 4-5 fresh lemon balm leaves

- 1 cup boiling water
- 1 teaspoon honey or sweetener (adjust to taste)

Another excellent choice is **Ginger and Lemon Tea**. Slice a small piece of fresh ginger and add it to boiling water with a slice of lemon. Let it steep for about ten minutes, then strain and sweeten with honey. This tea is perfect for combating nausea and providing a gentle energy boost.

- 1-inch piece of ginger, thinly sliced
- 1 slice of lemon
- 1 cup water
- 2 teaspoons honey (adjust to taste)

Brewing methods can significantly affect the flavor and effectiveness of herbal teas. Water temperature is crucial; for most herbal teas, boiling water is ideal. However, more delicate herbs like chamomile and peppermint can benefit from slightly cooler water to preserve their subtle flavors. Steeping times also vary depending on the herb. Chamomile and lavender typically require about five minutes, while heartier herbs like ginger may need closer to ten minutes to release their flavors fully. Enhancing your teas with natural sweeteners like honey or agave syrup can add a pleasant touch of sweetness without overpowering the herbal notes.

While many herbs are safe and beneficial during pregnancy, some should be avoided. Licorice root is one such herb. It can raise blood pressure and potentially lead to other complications. Certain essential oils, even in small amounts, can be harmful during pregnancy. It's best to avoid teas containing essential oils unless they are specifically formulated for pregnant women. High doses of certain herbs, such as nettle or yellow dock, can pose risks. Always consult with your healthcare provider before introducing new herbs into your diet.

7.3 MOCKTAILS RICH IN VITAMINS AND MINERALS

Packing your mocktails with nutrient-rich ingredients can support fetal growth, enhance energy levels, and improve overall health. For instance, Vitamin A is essential for developing your baby's heart, lungs, kidneys, eyes, and bones. Vitamin C, on the other hand, helps form collagen, which is vital for your baby's skin, tendons, and bones. Iron supports the increase in blood volume during pregnancy, ensuring that both you and your baby get enough oxygen. Incorporating these vitamins and minerals into your mocktails allows you to make every sip count toward a healthier pregnancy.

One fantastic recipe to try is the **Carrot and Orange Blend**. Carrots contain beta-carotene, which your body converts into Vitamin A, providing a sweet and earthy flavor. Oranges are rich in Vitamin C, enhancing the body's ability to absorb iron from other foods. Juice two large carrots and two oranges, combine the juices in a glass over ice, and add a touch of honey if you prefer a sweeter drink. The bright orange color and fresh taste make this mocktail delightful and nutritious. It's perfect for a morning boost or an afternoon pick-me-up.

- 2 large carrots, juiced
- 2 oranges, juiced

- Ice cubes
- 1 teaspoon honey (optional)

Another nutrient-dense option is the **Spinach and Pineapple Cooler**. Spinach is an excellent source of iron and folate, both crucial during pregnancy. Pineapple adds a tropical sweetness and is rich in Vitamin C, which aids in iron absorption. To prepare this cooler, blend a handful of fresh spinach with a cup of pineapple chunks and a splash of coconut water. Strain the mixture if you prefer a smoother texture, or enjoy it as is for a more rustic feel. Serve over ice and garnish with a slice of pineapple for a refreshing and healthful drink. This delicious cooler provides a great way to sneak in some leafy greens.

- 1/2 cup fresh spinach
- 1 cup fresh pineapple chunks
- 1/2 cup coconut water
- Ice cubes
- Pineapple slice for garnish

For a drink that's both vibrant and packed with nutrients, try the **Beet and Berry Mix**. Beets are rich in folate, which is essential for preventing neural tube defects in your baby. Berries are high in antioxidants, which help protect your and your baby's cells from damage. To make this mix, blend a small cooked beet with a cup of mixed berries (such as strawberries, blueberries, and raspberries) and a splash of apple juice. Strain the mixture if desired, and serve over ice. This mocktail's deep, rich color is as appealing as its nutrient profile, making it a fantastic choice for any time of the day.

- 1 small cooked beet, peeled and chopped
- 1 cup mixed berries (strawberries, blueberries, raspberries)

- 1/2 cup apple juice
- Ice cubes
- Mint leaves or extra berries for garnish

Maximizing nutrient absorption from these mocktails involves a few simple strategies. Pairing Vitamin C with iron-rich foods can significantly enhance iron absorption. For example, the Spinach and Pineapple Cooler combines spinach, an iron-rich leafy green, with pineapple, which is high in Vitamin C. This pairing makes it easier for your body to absorb the iron from the spinach. Using fat-soluble vitamins with healthy fats is another practical approach. For instance, the Carrot and Orange Blend contains beta-carotene, a fat-soluble vitamin. Adding a small amount of healthy fat, such as a teaspoon of olive oil or a slice of avocado, can help your body absorb this nutrient more efficiently. Additionally, avoid consuming nutrient inhibitors like caffeine, which can interfere with vitamin and mineral absorption. Opt for these nutrient-dense mocktails instead, ensuring you get the most out of every ingredient.

While these mocktails contain essential vitamins and minerals, it's important to remember the role of prenatal vitamins in your overall nutrition. Prenatal vitamins meet the increased nutritional needs during pregnancy. They contain higher levels of folic acid, iron, and other vital nutrients that support your baby's development. Complementing your diet with these supplements ensures you have a balanced intake of all necessary nutrients. Always consult your healthcare provider before starting any new supplement to ensure it's appropriate for your needs. While these nutrient-rich mocktails provide substantial benefits, they should not replace prenatal vitamins. Instead, consider them a delicious and nutritious addition to your wellness plan.

Creating a variety of nutrient-dense mocktails can make your pregnancy journey more enjoyable and healthful. These drinks' vibrant flavors and colors make them a pleasure to consume, while their nutritional benefits support you and your growing baby. Incorporating ingredients rich in vitamins and minerals ensures that every sip contributes to your well-being. As you continue to explore the world of mocktails, remember that your choices can positively impact your health and your baby's development.

ADVANCED MIXOLOGY TECHNIQUES

Early in my culinary journey, I stumbled upon the power of infusions and syrups. I had some fresh rosemary and citrus peels lying around and steeped them in hot water. The resulting aroma was intoxicating, and the flavor was magical. This simple experiment opened my eyes to the endless possibilities of crafting unique and complex flavors from everyday ingredients. Now, let's dive into the world of infusions, syrups, and other advanced techniques, where you can turn simple mocktails into extraordinary experiences.

8.1 CRAFTING INFUSIONS AND SYRUPS

Infusions are a fantastic way to add depth and complexity to your mocktails. The process involves steeping various ingredients in liquid to extract their flavors. For instance, infusing herbs in water or tea can create a refreshing base for your drinks. To start, place fresh herbs like mint, basil, or rosemary in a pitcher of hot water. Let them steep for about 30 minutes to an hour, depending on the intensity of flavor you desire. Once the infusion is ready, strain the herbs, leaving you with a flavorful base for mocktails.

Creating fruit and spice infusions follows a similar process but adds more complexity. Imagine a blend of sliced oranges, cinnamon sticks, and cloves steeped in hot water. The citrus provides a bright, tangy note, while the spices add warmth and depth. Time and temperature are crucial in this process. For a more robust flavor, let the ingredients steep for an extended period, but be mindful not to overdo it, as some herbs and spices can become bitter. Try to achieve the perfect balance through practice.

Flavored syrups are another cornerstone of advanced mixology. They offer concentrated bursts of flavor that can elevate any mocktail. Start with a simple syrup base, a mixture of equal parts water and sugar, heated until the sugar dissolves. You can get creative by adding herbs, spices, or citrus zest. For example, add dried lavender flowers and honey to the simple syrup base. Simmer the mixture for about 10-15 minutes, then strain out the lavender flowers. This lavender honey syrup will keep in the refrigerator for up to two weeks.

Another delightful syrup is a ginger and cardamom infusion. Combine fresh ginger slices and crushed cardamom pods with the simple syrup base. Simmer until the syrup takes on a warm, spicy aroma, then strain. This syrup adds a zesty kick to any mocktail. A citrus and rosemary syrup is perfect for those who love a blend of herbal and citrus notes. Add fresh rosemary sprigs and citrus zest to the simple syrup, simmer, and strain.

Balancing sweet and bitter elements in syrups is an art in itself. Adjusting sugar levels is your first step. Too much sugar can overpower other flavors, while too little can leave your drink lacking. Incorporating acidic elements like lemon juice can help balance the sweetness and add a refreshing tartness. For instance, adding a touch of lemon juice to a vanilla bean and cinnamon syrup can create a well-rounded flavor profile that isn't too sweet.

Here are a few recipes to get you started:

- Lavender and Honey Syrup: Combine 1 cup of water, 1 cup of sugar, 2 tablespoons of dried lavender flowers, and 2 tablespoons of honey. Simmer for 10-15 minutes, then strain.
- Ginger and Cardamom Infusion: Mix 1 cup of water, 1 cup of sugar, 1/4 cup of sliced fresh ginger, and 5 crushed cardamom pods. Simmer for 15 minutes, then strain.
- Citrus and Rosemary Syrup: Combine 1 cup of water, 1 cup of sugar, 2 tablespoons of citrus zest (lemon, lime, or orange), and 3-4 rosemary sprigs. Simmer for 10 minutes and strain.
- Vanilla Bean and Cinnamon Syrup: Mix 1 cup of water, 1 cup of sugar, 1 vanilla bean (split and scraped), and 2 cinnamon sticks. Simmer for 15 minutes, then strain.
- Jasmine Tea Syrup: Boil 1 cup of water. Remove from heat and add 2 jasmine tea bags (or 2 teaspoons loose-leaf jasmine tea in an infuser). Steep for about 6 minutes. Remove the tea bags or infuser, and return the pan to medium heat. Stir in 1 cup of sugar until it fully dissolves.

For a more floral flavor, steep the tea longer or use an additional tea bag.

Crafting these infusions and syrups allows you to personalize your mocktails, adding layers of flavor that make each sip an experience. Whether you're a health-conscious individual, an event host, or a mixology enthusiast, these techniques offer endless possibilities for creativity and enjoyment.

8.2 ADVANCED GARNISHING TECHNIQUES

Garnishes are vital in transforming a simple mocktail into an extraordinary experience. They enhance the drink's visual appeal and flavor, making it more inviting and enjoyable. Imagine presenting a mocktail adorned with intricately carved fruit or a sprig of fresh herbs. The garnish adds a splash of color and complements the drink's flavors, creating a harmonious balance.

Creative garnishing methods can turn any drink into a work of art. Carving fruit into intricate shapes is one way to add a touch of elegance. For instance, you can carve apples into specific shapes or create melon balls for a playful touch. Another technique is creating herb bouquets. Bundle a few sprigs of fresh herbs like mint, basil, or rosemary, and tie them together with a small piece of twine. These bouquets look beautiful and release aromatic oils into the drink as you sip. Edible flowers like pansies, orchids, and marigolds can add color and a subtle floral note to your mocktail. These flowers are safe to eat and can make your drink look as good as it tastes.

Dehydrated garnishes are another fantastic way to add a unique touch to your mocktails. Dehydrating fruits and herbs preserves their flavors and gives them a delightful crunch. To dehydrate citrus slices, slice the fruit thinly and place the slices on a baking

sheet lined with parchment paper. Dry them in the oven at a low temperature (around 200°F) for several hours until completely dried. You can also use a dehydrator, which is often more efficient. Creating herb crisps follows a similar method. Lay the herbs flat on a baking sheet and dry them at a low temperature until they become crisp. Dehydrated garnishes kept in an airtight container can add a sophisticated touch to your mocktails whenever you need them.

Specific garnishing ideas can add flair and complexity to your drinks. Candied ginger slices are a delightful addition, providing a sweet and spicy kick. To make them, slice fresh ginger thinly, simmer in a simple syrup until tender, and then dry them on a cooling rack. Infused sugar rims can also elevate your mocktails. Mix sugar with citrus zest or finely chopped herbs and use it to rim the glass, adding an extra layer of flavor with each sip. Artistic fruit peel twists are another great garnish. Use a vegetable peeler to create long, thin strips of citrus peel, then twist them into spirals. These can be draped over the edge of the glass or floated on top of the drink for a visually attractive effect.

Garnishing is an art that allows you to express creativity and attention to detail. The right garnish can make your mocktail taste better and look exquisite, turning an ordinary drink into a memorable experience. Whether crafting a refreshing summer cooler or a warming winter brew, these advanced garnishing techniques will help you create drinks that delight the senses and impress your guests.

8.3 LAYERING AND PRESENTATION MASTERY

Layering can transform a simple drink into a visual masterpiece. It involves carefully pouring different liquids into a glass to create distinct, colorful layers. This technique enhances the mocktail's visual appeal and adds flavor complexity. Each sip can bring a new taste experience, thanks to the gradual progression of flavors. Imagine the joy of sipping a mocktail that starts with a tangy hit of citrus and ends with a sweet berry finish. The visual separation of ingredients creates a stunning effect, making your drink look as good as it tastes.

The key to successful layering lies in understanding the density of your ingredients. Heavier liquids, like syrups, should be poured first, followed by lighter liquids, like juices or sodas. Begin by filling your glass with the heaviest liquid, such as a flavored syrup. Next, use the back of a spoon to slowly pour the next layer over the previous one. This technique helps to deflect the liquid and prevent it from mixing too quickly. For instance, if you're layering with syrups and juices, start with a base of grenadine, then gently layer orange juice on top, followed by a lighter liquid like club soda. The result is a beautifully stratified drink that invites you to savor each layer.

Presentation mastery goes beyond just layering. The choice of glassware can elevate your mocktail from ordinary to extraordinary. Elegant glassware adds a touch of sophistication and allows the layers to shine through. Consider using tall, narrow glasses for drinks with multiple layers, as they help highlight the distinct bands of color. Incorporating color contrasts can make your drink visually striking. Pairing vibrant hues like deep reds with bright yellows creates a captivating visual effect. The strategic placement of garnishes further enhances the presentation. A well-placed mint sprig or a citrus twist can add the finishing touch, making your mocktail Instagram-worthy.

One of my favorite layered mocktail recipes is the **Sunset Mocktail**. Start with a base of grenadine syrup (see chapter 3.3, Shirley Temple), add ice to the glass, carefully layer orange juice on top, and finish with a splash of sparkling water. The result is a drink that mimics the colors of a beautiful sunset, with layers of red, orange, and clear sparkling water.

- 2 tablespoons grenadine syrup
- 1/2 cup fresh orange juice
- 1/4 cup sparkling water (club soda or soda water)
- Ice cubes
- Orange slice or cherry for garnish

Another delightful option is the **Layered Berry and Mint Cooler**. Begin with a base of berry puree, add a layer of mint-infused syrup, and top with sparkling water. The contrast between the deep berry color and the bright green of the mint creates a visually stunning drink.

- 1/2 cup mixed berry puree (blend fresh or frozen berries like strawberries, raspberries, and blueberries)
- 2 tablespoons mint-infused simple syrup (See Chapter 1.5)
- 1/2 cup sparkling water (club soda or soda water)
- Ice cubes

- Fresh mint leaves and berries for garnish

For a tropical twist, try the **Tropical Paradise** mocktail. Start with a layer of pineapple juice, add a layer of coconut milk, and finish with a splash of mango juice. The creamy coconut layer in the middle adds a delightful texture, while the vibrant yellow and orange layers evoke the feel of a tropical getaway.

- 1/2 cup pineapple juice
- 1/4 cup coconut milk
- 1/4 cup mango juice
- Ice cubes
- Pineapple wedge or mango slices for garnish

Layering and presentation mastery are not just about aesthetics but also enhance the drinking experience. Each layer offers a different flavor profile, making each sip a new adventure. Whether hosting a party or enjoying a quiet evening at home, mastering these techniques will help you create visually stunning and delicious mocktails.

8.4 FERMENTED AND PROBIOTIC MOCKTAILS

Fermented drinks, such as kombucha or ginger beer, are an excellent way to add unique flavors and health benefits to your mocktails. They introduce a fizzy, tart element and contribute to a healthy gut microbiome. Such probiotics are essential for maintaining a balanced digestive system and improving overall well-being and mental clarity. Try adding them to your recipes.

Probiotic ingredients can further enhance the health benefits of your mocktails. Kefir and yogurt are excellent sources of probiotics. You can blend them with fruits and herbs to create creamy, tangy drinks. Adding probiotic supplements is another way to boost the health quotient of your mocktails. These supplements come in various forms, like powders or capsules, and mix easily into your drinks. Combining these probiotics with fresh fruits and herbs improves the flavor and makes the drink more nutritious.

Let's explore some specific recipes that highlight fermented and probiotic ingredients. This **Citrus Kombucha Cooler** is fizzy, tangy, and packed with refreshing citrus flavors, perfect for a bright and healthy drink. In a glass or cocktail shaker, combine the fresh orange juice, lemon juice, and honey or agave syrup (if using). Stir or shake well to blend. Pour in the kombucha and gently stir to mix. Fill a glass with ice cubes and pour the kombucha mixture over the ice. Garnish with slices of orange and lemon and a sprig of fresh mint for a pop of color and freshness.

- 1/2 cup citrus-flavored kombucha (or your favorite flavor)
- 1/4 cup fresh orange juice
- 1/4 cup fresh lemon juice
- 1 tablespoon honey or agave syrup (optional for sweetness)
- Ice cubes
- Orange and lemon slices for garnish
- Fresh mint leaves for garnish

This **Spiced Ginger Mojito** is refreshing and zesty, with a perfect balance of spicy ginger and tangy lime, ideal for a sophisticated, non-alcoholic option. In a glass or shaker, gently muddle the mint leaves with fresh lime juice and honey (or simple syrup), releasing the mint's oils for flavor. Fill the glass with ice cubes, then pour in the ginger beer. Stir well to mix. For a lighter drink, top with a splash of sparkling water. Garnish with a lime wedge and a sprig of fresh mint.

- 1/2 cup ginger beer
- 1/4 cup fresh lime juice
- 1 tablespoon honey or simple syrup (optional for added sweetness)
- 8-10 fresh mint leaves
- Sparkling water (optional for a lighter drink)
- Ice cubes
- Lime wedges and mint sprigs for garnish

For a creamy delight, try the **Kefir and Mango Cooler.** Blend kefir with fresh mango chunks and a bit of honey, then serve over ice. This drink is both tangy and sweet, perfect for a hot day.

- 1 cup kefir (plain or lightly sweetened)
- 1 cup fresh mango chunks
- 1 tablespoon honey (adjust to taste)
- Ice cubes
- Mango slices for garnish

Finally, the **Probiotic Apple and Cinnamon Blend** combines apple juice with cinnamon and a probiotic supplement. This mocktail is simple, delicious, and beneficial for your gut health.

- 1 cup apple juice (preferably fresh or 100% natural)
- 1 teaspoon ground cinnamon (or a small cinnamon stick)
- 1 probiotic capsule or powder (follow the serving instructions on your probiotic supplement)
- Ice cubes (optional)
- Apple slices for garnish

Experimenting with fermented and probiotic ingredients opens up a world of flavors and health benefits. Whether you're a mom with kids, a mixology enthusiast, or someone looking to improve your gut health, these mocktails offer a delightful way to enjoy taste and wellness.

8.6 THE ROLE OF TEXTURE IN MOCKTAILS

Texture is an often-overlooked element that can profoundly impact the enjoyment of a mocktail. Imagine sipping a creamy coconut and pineapple blend on a hot summer day. The smooth, velvety texture enhances the mouthfeel, making each sip a luxurious experience. Texture adds depth and interest, transforming a simple drink into a multi-sensory delight. Balancing different textures within a mocktail can add complexity, making each sip unique and intriguing.

Various ingredients contribute to the texture of mocktails. Creamy elements like coconut milk and yogurt add a rich, smooth, indulgent, and satisfying texture. These ingredients can transform any fruit blend into a creamy, dreamy mocktail. Fizzy elements, such as sparkling water and soda, introduce a lively, effervescent texture that can make a drink feel refreshing and vibrant. The bubbles dance on your tongue, adding a playful element to the drink. Thickening agents like chia seeds and xanthan gum can add body and a slight chewiness, creating a more substantial drink that feels nourishing and filling.

Here are some recipes that highlight different textural elements. The **Creamy Coconut and Pineapple Blend** combines coconut milk, fresh pineapple chunks, and a bit of honey. Blend until smooth and serve chilled. This drink offers a rich, creamy texture, perfect for a hot day.

- 1 cup fresh pineapple chunks
- 1/2 cup coconut milk (full-fat for creaminess)
- 1 tablespoon honey (adjust to taste)
- Ice cubes (optional)
- Pineapple slice for garnish

The **Thick and Fruity Chia Seed Smoothie** combines fresh berries, yogurt, and chia seeds. Blend the berries and yogurt, then stir in the chia seeds and let sit for a few minutes to create a thick, flavorful smoothie with a delightful chewiness.

- 1/2 cup fresh or frozen mixed berries
- 1/2 cup yogurt (plain or flavored, Greek yogurt for extra thickness)
- 1 tablespoon chia seeds
- 1 teaspoon honey or maple syrup
- 1/2 cup almond milk (or any milk of choice)
- Fresh berries for garnish

These techniques and recipes show how texture can add a new dimension to your mocktails, making them delicious, engaging, and satisfying. Mastering the role of texture in mocktails can elevate your drink-making skills and enhance the overall drinking experience.

8.7 UNDERSTANDING ACIDITY AND BALANCE IN DRINKS

Acidity is a vital component in crafting balanced mocktails. It brightens flavors, provides a refreshing quality, and balances sweetness, creating a more complex and enjoyable drink. When you sip a perfectly balanced mocktail, acidity often gives it that crisp, clean finish, leaving you wanting more. The right level of acidity can transform a flat, one-dimensional drink into a vibrant, multi-layered experience. For instance, a touch of lemon juice in a berry mocktail can elevate the natural sweetness of the berries, making each sip more refreshing and satisfying.

There are several sources of acidity that you can use to enhance your mocktails. Citrus juices like lemon, lime, and orange are the most common and versatile. They add a bright, tangy note that pairs well with various flavors. Vinegar, such as apple cider or balsamic, offers different acidity. They bring a sharp, tangy taste with a slightly sweet undertone, adding complexity to your drinks. Fermented ingredients like kombucha and kefir contribute acidity while adding unique flavor and health benefits. These ingredients can make your mocktails more exciting and beneficial for gut health.

Balancing acidity in your mocktails is crucial for creating a harmonious drink. A splash of citrus juice can add the necessary brightness to balance sweetness. If your mocktail feels too sharp, adding a touch of sweetness can help counterbalance the acidity. For instance, a bit of honey or agave syrup can mellow out the tartness of lemon juice, creating a more rounded flavor. Experimenting with different acidic ingredients can also help you find the perfect balance. Try combining citrus juices with a splash of vinegar or fermented liquid to see how these flavors interact and enhance each other.

The **Apple Cider Vinegar Tonic** is a great example. Mix apple cider vinegar with honey, water, and lemon juice. The honey tempers the vinegar's sharpness, while the lemon juice adds an extra layer of brightness.

- 1 tablespoon apple cider vinegar
- 1 teaspoon honey (adjust to taste)
- 1 tablespoon fresh lemon juice
- 1 cup water (cold or warm, depending on your preference)
- Ice cubes (optional for a cold version)
- Lemon slice for garnish

Perfecting the acidity balance in your mocktails will enhance your drink-making abilities, enabling you to craft tasty and invigorating beverages with a layered depth of flavor.

CONCLUSION

As we conclude our journey through the fascinating world of mocktails, let's reflect on the vibrant array of recipes we've explored together. Each chapter has introduced you to new flavors and techniques that can transform simple ingredients into delightful non-alcoholic beverages, from refreshing coolers and creamy shakes to herbal infusions and sparkling blends.

Throughout this book, we've emphasized the importance of using simple, accessible, and healthy ingredients. Fresh fruits, herbs, natural sweeteners, and sparkling waters have been our key components, ensuring that every mocktail is not only delicious but also beneficial for your health. We've celebrated nature's bounty in every sip by focusing on these wholesome ingredients.

We've also delved into various mixology techniques, from the foundational skills of muddling, shaking, and stirring to more advanced methods like infusions and layering. Whether you're preparing a quick and easy mocktail for last-minute guests or crafting an intricate drink for a special occasion, the skills you've gained will serve you well.

Our exploration has included ideas for family-friendly, pregnancy-safe, and large event mocktails. By considering the needs and preferences of different groups, we've ensured that everyone can enjoy these delightful beverages. Family gatherings, baby showers, birthdays, and holidays can all be elevated with the right mocktail, making these moments even more memorable.

Sustainability and seasonality have been recurring themes, highlighting the importance of using seasonal and locally sourced ingredients. This approach enhances your mocktails' flavors and nutritional value, supports local farmers, and reduces your environmental footprint.

We've discussed the art of flavor pairings, the health benefits of various ingredients, the balance of acidity, and the role of texture in creating well-rounded drinks. By understanding these elements, you can craft perfectly balanced and exceptionally satisfying mocktails.

Presentation and garnishing play a crucial role in enhancing the drinking experience. A well-garnished mocktail is visually appealing and invites guests to savor every sip. You can elevate even the most straightforward drinks with thoughtful touches like citrus twists, herb sprigs, and edible flowers.

I've encouraged you to experiment with flavors and create personalized mocktails that reflect your tastes and creativity. The recipes and techniques provided are just the starting point. Your imagination is the only limit to what you can create.

CONCLUSION | 141

Choosing a sober lifestyle has numerous benefits, and mocktails can support this choice by offering satisfying and sophisticated alternatives to alcoholic beverages. By embracing mocktails, you can enjoy social gatherings, improve your health, and stay present in every moment.

As you embark on your mocktail-making journey, I invite you to use the recipes and tips in this book as a foundation. Share your creations and experiences on social media using the hashtag **#MocktailsMadeEasy**. Hosting a mocktail party is a beautiful way to share the joy of non-alcoholic drinks with friends and family.

Continue to explore new ingredients and flavors, and don't hesitate to experiment beyond the book. Your creativity and curiosity will lead you to discover even more delightful combinations.

Thank you for joining me on this journey. It has been a privilege to share my passion for mocktails with you, and I hope this book has inspired you to embrace a healthier, more creative, and joyful lifestyle.

Remember, mocktails are about the experiences, connections, and positive changes they can bring to your life. Find joy and fulfillment in the art of mocktail making, and let every sip be a celebration of health, creativity, and gratitude.

Cheers to a life filled with beautiful, delicious, and uplifting mocktails!

Now that you've got everything you need to craft incredible mocktails, it's time to share your newfound skills with others! By leaving your honest review of Mocktails Made Easy on Amazon, you'll help fellow drink lovers discover the joy of creating their own refreshing beverages.

Your review will show other readers where they can find easy, delicious mocktail recipes, helping them add flavor and fun to any occasion—just like you have.

Thank you for being part of this flavorful journey! The art of mocktail-making thrives when we share our knowledge, and with your review, you're helping to do just that.

Warmly,

- Eric Santagada

Scan the QR code below

REFERENCES

Sobreo. (n.d.). *The history of mocktails.* https://sobreo.com/blogs/california-cocktails-blog/the-history-of-mocktails

Aspen Valley Hospital. (n.d.). *The positive effects of sobriety on your health.* https://www.aspenhospital.org/healthy-journey/the-positive-effects-of-sobriety-on-your-health/

The Bar. (n.d.). *Create delicious mocktail recipes with must-have tools and ingredients.* https://in.thebar.com/articles/create-delicious-mocktail-recipes-with-must-have-tools-and-ingredients

Flavorsum. (n.d.). *Free from alcohol, full of flavor.* https://flavorsum.com/free-from-alcohol-full-of-flavor/

Prairie View A&M University. (2016). *Health benefits of infused water.* https://www.pvamu.edu/cafnr/2016/05/24/health-benefits-of-infused-water/

Mountain Rose Herbs. (n.d.). *How to build a home mocktail bar + recipes.* https://blog.mountainroseherbs.com/how-to-build-a-home-mocktail-bar-with-mocktail-recipes

Scientific Direct. (n.d.). *Fruit and vegetable-based beverages—Nutritional benefits.* https://www.sciencedirect.com/science/article/pii/B9780128166895000110

Trufoo Juice Bar. (n.d.). *25 best superfoods to add to your smoothie for a nutrient boost.* https://www.trufoojuicebar.co.uk/single-post/25-best-superfoods-to-add-to-your-smoothie-for-a-nutrient-boost

Ally's Kitchen. (n.d.). *The powerful health benefits of fresh herbs.* https://allyskitchen.com/health-benefits-of-fresh-herbs/

Time Out. (n.d.). *15 best farmer's markets in Philadelphia for fresh produce.* https://www.timeout.com/philadelphia/shopping/farmers-markets-in-philadelphia

Carman, T. (2022, July 29). *How to store fresh herbs to keep them perky and happy.* The Washington Post. https://www.washingtonpost.com/food/2022/07/29/how-to-store-fresh-herbs/#:

Brit + Co. (n.d.). *31 must-try spring mocktails: Floral & fruity!.* https://www.brit.co/food/cocktails/spring-mocktails/

Kim, M., Han, J., Kim, J., Kang, S., Kim, D., & Seol, G. H. (2022). *Citrus essential oils in aromatherapy: Therapeutic effects.* Integrative Medicine Research, *11*(1), 100872. https://www.ncbi.nlm.nih.gov/pmc/articles/PMC9774566/

Srivastava, J. K., Shankar, E., & Gupta, S. (2010). *Chamomile: A herbal medicine of the past with bright future. Molecular Medicine Reports, 3*(6), 895-901. https://www.ncbi.nlm.nih.gov/pmc/articles/PMC2995283/

Archie Juice. (n.d.). *The powerful trio: Benefits of cayenne pepper, turmeric, and ginger.* https://archiejuice.com/blogs/what-is-a-cold-pressed-juice/the-powerful-trio-benefits-of-cayenne-pepper-turmeric-and-ginger#:

Through the Fibro Fog. (n.d.). *Cucumber mint mocktail.* https://www.throughthefibrofog.com/cucumber-mint-mocktail/

Bon Appétit. (n.d.). *29 mocktail recipes worthy of a second round.* https://www.bonappetit.com/gallery/best-mocktail-recipes

Chef Bai. (n.d.). *The Life Jacket Pitcher (large batch summer mocktails).* https://www.chefbai.kitchen/blog/lifejacketmocktail

The Mixer. (n.d.). *11 refreshing mocktails to serve at brunch.* https://www.themixer.com/en-us/trends/brunch-mocktails/

The Three Drinkers. (n.d.). *Mocktail presentation ideas — Spirits.* https://www.thethreedrinkers.com/magazine-content/tag/Mocktail+presentation+ideas

One Sweet Appetite. (n.d.). *Fruit punch recipe (non-alcoholic).* https://onesweetappetite.com/fruit-punch-recipe-non-alcoholic/

Rainbow Delicious. (2024). *25 unique lemonade recipes to try in 2024.* https://rainbowdelicious.com/unique-lemonade-recipes/

Kaiser Permanente. (n.d.). *Healthy smoothies for kids.* https://about.kaiserpermanente.org/health-and-wellness/recipes/healthy-smoothies-for-kids

The First Year Blog. (n.d.). *Miami Vice mocktail popsicles.* https://thefirstyearblog.com/miami-vice-mocktail-popsicles/

All About Women. (n.d.). *What are the benefits of eating citrus during pregnancy?* https://blog.allaboutwomenmd.com/pregnancy-prenatal-care/benefits-of-citrus-pregnancy.htm

American Pregnancy Association. (n.d.). *Herbal tea & pregnancy: A handbook for expecting mothers.* https://americanpregnancy.org/healthy-pregnancy/is-it-safe/herbal-tea/

Pregnant & Hungry. (n.d.). *Nutritious mocktail recipes for pregnancy and postpartum.* https://pregnantandhungry.com/category/pregnancy/mocktails/

American Pregnancy Association. (n.d.). *Pregnancy smoothies.* https://americanpregnancy.org/healthy-pregnancy/pregnancy-health-wellness/pregnancy-smoothies/

Delish. (2023). *34 best Christmas mocktails: Holiday non-alcoholic drinks.* https://www.delish.com/holiday-recipes/christmas/g42063143/non-alcoholic-christmas-drinks/

The Knot. (n.d.). *25 festive wedding mocktails that pack a punch.* https://www.theknot.com/content/mocktail-ideas

Town & Country. (n.d.). *12 best New Year's Eve mocktails.* https://www.townandcountrymag.com/leisure/drinks/g3127/new-years-eve-mocktails/

Tasting Table. (2024). *15 summer mocktails to elevate your BBQ.* https://www.tastingtable.com/1301139/summer-mocktails-elevate-bbq/

McBride, K. (n.d.). *How to make herbal water.* https://kamimcbride.com/how-to-make-herbal-water/

Moody Mixologist. (n.d.). *The art of the cocktail garnish.* https://www.moodymixologist.com/blog/the-art-of-the-cocktail-garnish

Diageo Bar Academy. (n.d.). *The art of layering in cocktails.* https://www.diageobaracademy.com/en-us/home/customer-service/the-art-of-layering-in-cocktails#:

Harvard Health Publishing. (n.d.). *Fermented foods can add depth to your diet.* https://www.health.harvard.edu/staying-healthy/fermented-foods-can-add-depth-to-your-diet

Made in the USA
Columbia, SC
16 March 2025